W9-CNJ-972

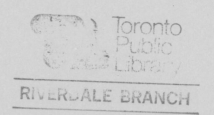
Toronto
Public
Library

RIVERDALE BRANCH

Lessons from the
GOLF GREATS

Toronto
Public
Library

RIVERDALE BRANCH

Lessons from the
GOLF GREATS

David Leadbetter

with Richard Simmons

Foreword by
Peter Dobereiner

Sequence photography by
DAVE CANNON

Illustrations by
DAVE F. SMITH

HarperCollinsPublishersLtd

Dedication: To the great players of the game past and present; to the
weekenders, the fanatics, the scientists, the teachers, the historians, the administrators,
the writers, the students, the architects and the course care-takers. To whoever picked up a club and
accepted the challenge, I give tribute to you for making this game of golf what it is. I give thanks for me being
a part of it, and it is my hope that my children and yours grow up in this modern high-tech world with an
understanding and appreciation for the game that will at least give them a link with the past, and an
awareness of the traditions, morals and virtues of yesteryear to help guide them in the future.
To my Kelly, God bless you. **David Leadbetter**

LESSONS FROM THE GOLF GREATS
Copyright © 1995 by David Leadbetter

All rights reserved. No part of this book may be used or reproduced
in any manner whatsoever without prior written permission
except in the case of brief quotations embodied in reviews.
For information, address HarperCollins Publishers Ltd, Suite 2900,
Hazelton Lanes, 55 Avenue Road, Toronto, Canada M5R 3L2.

First published in 1995 by CollinsWillow an imprint of
HarperCollins*Publishers*, London

First Canadian edition by HarperCollins Publishers Ltd: 1995

A CIP catalogue record for this book is available from the
National Library of Canada.

ISBN 0-00-255407-0

Designed and produced by
Cooling Brown (*Book Packaging*), Hampton, Middlesex, England

Color Reproduction by
Saxon Design Services, Norwich, England

Printed in Italy

95 96 97 98 99 AP 10 9 8 7 6 5 4 3 2 1

CONTENTS

FOREWORD

I have lost count, and forgotten some of the names, of the new messiahs of golf theory who have burst upon the scene, who have briefly held our rapt attention before returning to well deserved obscurity when pointing the chin at the right knee at address – or was it the left knee? – failed to turn us all into scratch golfers. Bring on the next messiah!

David Leadbetter does not fit into this pattern of the fashionable teacher of the moment. For many years he was golf's best kept secret, hugely respected by a select group of tournament professionals but unknown to the world of golf at large. The trouble was, he didn't have a gimmick, and still hasn't, but his clients started dominating the major championships. Now he is the best known teacher in the world and everyone with a fat wallet and a thin talent is chasing him for his secret. He does not have one of those either.

He is an adept diagnostician (as are many others) and has a profound knowledge of the golf swing (as do many others). What sets him apart is his genius for communication. Most golf instruction is conducted in technical jargon, or gibberish as it should more properly be designated. Example: Stand at the address and rotate your hands ten degrees in a clockwise direction. The clubface is now said to be 'open'. Perform this identical movement when at the top of the backswing and the clubface is now said to be 'shut'. No wonder the student's eyes glaze over. Ernest Jones, a pioneer guru back in the twenties, called it 'Paralysis through Analysis'.

I don't think David Leadbetter even cares whether his students understand the effect of centripetal force on clubhead acceleration. He gets them hitting the ball farther and straighter just by telling them what to do in simple and graphic terms. Moreover, his enthusiasm for his mission of making you into a better golfer is infectious. When he gets you hitting them flush off the screws he gets an even bigger charge of satisfaction than you do.

That enthusiasm and gift of communication illuminates every page of this splendid book to provide you with a fascinating insight into the workings of the golf swing. It is no easy task selecting just twenty five of the world's greatest contemporary players, but David Leadbetter has drawn on his vast experience to present a detailed study of some of the game's most distinctive styles, this unique format enabling him to pull out specific points that can benefit your own game. Enjoy it for what it is, a jolly good read, and you may well find that the experience makes you a better golfer. Quite a trick, that.

PETER DOBEREINER

INTRODUCTION
A study in technique

For as long as I can remember I have enjoyed studying picture sequences of the games greatest players, fascinated at the individual interpretation that each and every one has made successful. In that respect I consider myself as much a student as a teacher of the golf swing. And as surely as I continue to learn about and understand this game, so my philosophy will continue to be developed.

Throughout my career I have been an avid collector of magazine articles and books on the subject of instruction. Certain volumes date from the 19th century, and to compare images of the way the game was played then with the way it is played today is to appreciate how the swing has evolved through the ages. After much study and debate on this matter with the many players I have been fortunate enough to work with, the one conclusion I can draw with any degree of certainty is that there is no *definitive* method. The ultimate definition is that a good swing is not one necessarily pleasing to the eye, but one that *repeats* and rewards the player with control over the flight of the ball.

In writing this book I wanted to capture the essence of the golf swing within the perspective of the modern era, which I have defined as dating from 1980 onwards. I wanted to present a broad spectrum of the world's current crop of leading players, but including a few past stars who are still dominant in the world of professional golf. Thus the majority of players featured within these pages have won major championships; those who have not yet achieved that honour I believe have the potential to do so.

From an historical point of view it would have been fascinating to include such influential players of the golden era as Harry Vardon, J H Taylor and James Braid – the so-called *Great Triumvirate*. Had space allowed I would also have enjoyed analysing the legendary swings of Walter Hagen, Gene Sarazen and Bobby Jones. Should such an opportunity ever arise again I would add to that list the names of Mickey Wright – one of the greatest women

golfers and finest swingers of our time – along with Ben Hogan, Byron Nelson, Sam Snead, Henry Cotton, Bobby Locke, Roberto de Vicenzo, Julius Boros, Australia's Peter Thompson, Gary Player and Arnold Palmer. I only wish there had been room enough to also include an analysis of Tony Jacklin, Tom Weiskopf, Johnny Miller, Hubert Green, David Graham and Japan's Isao Aoki.

Many other contemporary players are conspicuous by their absence, and I am sure that between the time of writing and the date of publication a new star will emerge – or an old star re-emerge – and stamp his or her authority on the game. Such is life. Looking at the current crop of established players, I would like to have featured Mark Calcavecchia, Ben Crenshaw, Steve Elkington, Sandy Lyle, Larry Mize, Tommy Nakajima, Larry Nelson, Jumbo Ozaki, Corey Pavin, Scott Simpson, Vijay Singh, Craig Stadler, Lanny Wadkins and Fuzzy Zoeller. All of these players have influenced the game, the way it is taught, and the way it is played.

In my commentary, I have tried to be entirely objective, highlighting individual traits and strengths in each case and drawing attention to the natural differences that exist. Like fingerprints, no two swings are exactly the same (no two *body types* are exactly the same), and indeed what might be considered the perfect swing for one player will not necessarily apply to another. However it is possible to identify certain principles that define a dynamic, repeating swing: *key elements* such as the set-up position, the pivot motion (i.e. the transfer of weight in harmony with the turning of the body), a consistent plane tied with a good wrist action, and the subsequent use of centrifugal force. All of these elements combine to give a player clubhead control.

Once you have enjoyed viewing the swings of these great players, you will find what I have described as 'worksheets'. In these worksheets I have endeavoured to focus on one or two aspects of that particular player's swing that I felt were *key* ingredients in their ability to strike the ball; keys that hopefully might be incorporated into benefiting your own technique. These are the practical keys, drills and exercises I use in my teaching when tailoring instruction to an individual.

Learning to swing a golf club is not just about following a perfect model. Once you have read the book and accumulated a little technical know-how, don't be afraid to experiment with trial and error. That's all part of the fun of learning. You may well find that two or three different thoughts are suggested to benefit one specific move – for example, in the all-important change of direction from backswing to downswing. My hope is that with a range of ideas and sensations to experiment with, one might strike home. As you study the pictures, try to build an image of the swing that suits *you*. Focus on the players of a similar height and build to yourself, then work towards those images on the practice tee.

Is there such a thing as a technically perfect swing? If there is, I have yet to see it. Certain players are perhaps closer to an ideal than others, and once in a while a player might have found the 'secret' for a string of holes, but none has achieved total perfection. The human element just does not allow it – and there is so much more to this game than having a good swing. What is clear is that every great player has the intuitive sense of *feel* necessary to compensate for the fact that his or her swing is flawed in some way. And such is their skill, they are able to repeat that compensation to strike the ball squarely, time after time. Based on a sound appreciation of the fundamentals – i.e. the set-up, the coiling motion, balance and rhythm – they are able to swing the clubhead on a

consistent plane and path, and accelerate through the ball confident that the clubface is square as it tracks the target.

With the advent of high-speed photography and video analysis, we are now better equipped than ever before to study the swing and make comparisons. But remember this: *the pictures you see contained within these pages capture positions within motion.* The one failing any book of this nature must suffer is that it can not fully impress upon you the overall rhythm and timing of a good swing – that intangible quality. There is a great amount of feel and artistry involved, and in that respect some golfers are naturally more talented than others.

However, of this I am certain. The quality of one's technique is borne out by the way the ball is struck and flies through the air, and without exception the players you see featured in the pages of this book have qualities that have been tested under the severest of pressure – the arena of professional tournament golf. In acknowledging their achievements, I would like finally to thank each one for teaching me and broadening my horizons, so that I might share and pass on some of that knowledge to you.

DAVID LEADBETTER

PAUL AZINGER

BORN: JANUARY 6TH, 1960, HOLYOKE, MASSACHUSETTS, USA. **TURNED PRO:** 1981. **HEIGHT:** 6ft 2in (1.9m).

Determined. Courageous. A fighter. A man without fear who does not back off a challenge. A man whose single-minded tenacity glares most in a head-to-head situation. Such as in the Ryder Cup matches, where his game seems to move into a higher gear. A man who responds well to pressure. All of these qualities we associated with Paul Azinger before he underlined them in overcoming his illness in 1994.

The 'Zinger', as he is known on tour, was not a great amateur player. He first picked up a club when he was four years old and yet could not break 80 until the senior years at college in Florida. One summer, taking a range job at Arnold Palmer's Bay Hill Club, he was able to hit balls all day long, and as he improved he nurtured not just a unique, repeating swing, but a deadly competitive instinct. A late bloomer, once he realised the depth of his potential – thanks to the encouragement of his father, a retired lieutenant colonel – he turned pro, and honed his game on the tough Florida mini-tour circuit.

More than anything, Paul has focused on one goal: to *control* the flight of the golf ball. Technically speaking, his swing may not appeal to the purist, but it is simple and it *repeats*. Employing perhaps the strongest of grips in the modern game, Paul is respected by his peers for the quality of his ball-striking, and has great feel for punching half and three-quarter shots, 'knocking' the ball down under the wind. He is what I describe as a 'shut-face' player; one who closes the clubface in the process of making his backswing, and

Paul Azinger is congratulated by Seve Ballesteros after a record 62 during the 1994 Johnnie Walker World Championship at the Tryall Club, Jamaica.

who then compensates with a supreme effort to rotate and clear his body on the way down, so that he is able to return the clubface square to slightly open through impact. This he does beautifully to produce a controlled left to right shape – a fade.

On top of all this, Paul is blessed with a superlative short game. He has a particularly fine touch with the wedge and judges distance to the inch. Statistically, he ranks as one of the world's leading bunker players, and under pressure is just as useful with the putter. If he has a weakness, it could be that he does tend to flight the ball low to the ground. In the mould of Lee Trevino, he is most at home on hard and fast links-type courses, where the skill lies in working the ball with the natural lie of the land. Any course that demands high-flying approach shots – most notably Augusta National – is for him a tougher proposition.

Paul won his first tournament – the Phoenix Open – in January of 1987, and six months later might easily have won the British Open at Muirfield had he been more used to being in contention in a Major championship. Professional sportsmen talk about a learning process that yields a tough mental edge, and the Muirfield experience sparked a streak in which he won for seven straight years on the PGA tour, earning over $6 million in official winnings. More than money, Paul Azinger's all-round talent and bravery deserved major recognition, and none in recent years was more popular than his play-off victory over Greg Norman in the 1993 US PGA Championship at Inverness.

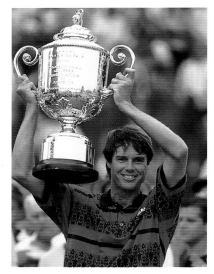

Winning the 1993 US PGA at Inverness Golf Club, Ohio.

Proving that unorthodox technique can stand up to the heat of even the most pressure-laden competition, Paul Azinger should provide inspiration in terms of working with what you've got.

The swing:
active body, passive hands

The most talked about feature of Paul Azinger's make-up as a player is that he employs a very strong grip. Both of his hands are turned well to the right on the club (as he looks at it), and the V-formed between the thumb and forefinger on his right hand points well to the outside of his right shoulder (**1**). A natural low-ball player, Paul also tends to position the ball towards the rear part of his stance, and for the majority of his shots sets up in such a way that his left arm and the clubshaft are comfortably aligned. Here, with a 5-iron, the rear view confirms the slightly 'open' look of the lower body.

As he draws the club away (**2**), Paul extends his left arm and moves his head slightly off the ball in unison – a key point in this swing. With a relatively slow and controlled tempo, he makes a fairly early shoulder turn (**3**), then completes his backswing with a further rotation of his hips and chest and a raising of the arms – a most deliberate turning action that gets him fully wound up at the top, yet with very much a three-quarter length swing (**4**).

Paul compensates for his strong grip and shut clubface position with what he describes as a *'level'* feeling backswing, the emphasis being on turning the hips and shoulders. The right leg is forced to straighten from its original position at address as he rotates his body, and the left heel rises slightly up off the ground as he reaches the top.

Down the line you can see this clearly, and it is interesting to observe that Paul turns his shoulders on a flat plane, matched by an equally flat left arm plane. This is unusual for a tall player: ordinarily you would expect to see the left

1

2

3

4

arm swing more upright than the shoulder plane, but it does reward Paul with a very 'connected' looking swing.

Instinctively aware of the severely shut clubface at the top, Paul makes an emphatic lateral motion, sliding his knees towards the target as he starts down (**5**). At the same time, look at the way he retains his wrist cock: to guard against hooking the ball, his right elbow works in close to his side, towards the right hip.

The angle held between the shaft and right wrist provides great speed through impact when the clubhead is finally released and catches up with the hands – the impact position featuring a virtual mirror-image of the hands/clubhead relationship as set at address (**6**).

As he approaches impact, Paul is concerned about one thing: clearing the left side of his body. Having driven his knees towards the target he can be seen to rotate

his hips aggressively out of the way, as a result of which his torso is noticeably open (i.e. pointing left of the target) through the ball (**7**). A split-second after the left side of his body has cleared, the whole of his right side 'fires', and the full force of the swing is released.

Paul Azinger epitomises what I describe as the *'body release'* type of player. The emphasis here is on the rotary motion of the body and having generated great speed he winds up in a well-balanced finish,

with his spine relatively straight and his chest facing the target (**8**).

If we examine the follow through we can see that the hands are relatively passive – there is no 'cross-over' through the ball. The toe of the club is not allowed to pass the heel, so even with that strong grip he creates left-to-right spin. In this swing, the hands are always *leading* the clubhead, which explains why Paul is such an excellent punch player in the wind.

5

6

7

8

What you can learn from Paul Azinger's swing

LESSON ONE: BROOM-HANDLE DRILL REPLACES TILT WITH A TURN

A lot of golfers remark at how easily good players seem to generate power. The reason they are able to do this is that they make a good turning motion *behind* the ball on the backswing, and so maximise their coil and wind-up.

By far the simplest way to ensure making a full turn is to rotate the shoulders on a fairly level plane (Paul Azinger being a prime example), as opposed to tilting them downwards. Such a tilting motion of the shoulders plagues many golfers, especially when they try to keep their head 'dead still'. This misnomer results in a lack of motion, a faulty transfer of weight, and leads to

the club being 'picked up' to produce a choppy type of swing. And while you can get away with this with the shorter clubs, such a fault leads to a great loss of distance and direction with the longer irons and woods.

The exercise you see here will help to familiarise you with the sensation of the proper turning motion. Start by placing a

broom-handle behind your back, hooked between your elbows, then assume your normal posture, and rehearse the pivot: turn back so that an extension of the broom handle and your shoulders would look out *beyond* the ball. [Under no circumstances should the broom handle or your shoulders look down at the ball.]

With practice, this exercise will give you the feeling of turning your shoulders on a more level axis. This will automatically free up your body motion, and promote a swing in which the club travels more *around* your body – exactly what you need to sweep the ball away with the longer clubs.

This broom-handle drill is also a great stretching exercise for the big back muscles, and as such is particularly beneficial to senior golfers who may lack flexibility. The key is to sense that you turn your shoulders first away from and then towards the target on a fairly symmetrical angle to get the feeling of the whole swing.

And don't worry if your head moves a little as you rehearse this drill. Most great players display a little lateral motion of the head – especially with the longer clubs.

LESSON TWO: BALL ABOVE FEET PROMOTES ROUNDED SWING, POWERFUL RELEASE

While his natural shape is a fade, Paul Azinger does not swing the club from outside-to-in to produce this shot. With a good rotary body action, the clubhead is always approaching the ball from inside the target line, and that's the key to powerful and consistent hitting.

If you are a slicer or a puller of the ball – i.e. an *out-to-in* swinger (you can check this by looking at your divots; they will point to the left of the target) – one way to familiarise yourself with the proper feeling of swinging from the inside is to hit shots off a sidehill lie, the ball positioned several inches above the level of your feet.

Not only will this exercise help to level out your shoulder turn, but it will also give you a more rounded, flatter swing plane (slicers suffer a *steep* swing plane coming into the ball). Repeat this often enough, and the resulting shallow angle of approach will promote the more desirable inside-to-out swingpath through the ball. And if you release the clubhead properly, you will soon cultivate a draw, and a divot pattern that looks towards your target.

Paul Azinger fades the ball primarily because he employs such a strong grip and with it retains the angle in his wrists to hold the clubface square to slightly open in relation to the target line through the ball. Most golfers would be better off trying to promote a draw for the simple reason the right to left shape maximises distance. If you practise from a sidehill lie, and get the feeling of releasing the club by allowing the hands to crossover naturally, you will soon enjoy striking the ball solidly.

SEVE BALLESTEROS

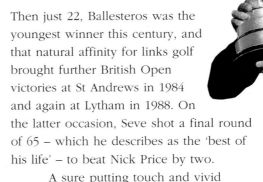

BORN: APRIL 9TH, 1957, PEDRENA, SPAIN. **TURNED PRO:** 1974. **HEIGHT:** 6ft (1.8m).

Severiano Ballesteros grew up beside the seaside course of Pedrena, in northern Spain, where his uncle, the great Ramon Sota, was the professional. Along with his brothers, Seve worked as a caddie, stealing whatever hours he could to play the game he loved. Several pictures of a smiling young champion adorn the walls of the old wooden clubhouse, which overlooks the bay, and many of the older members can recall the figure of a boy on the beach, inventing shots with a rusty iron and a few old balls in the last evening light. They witnessed the making of a legend.

A professional at 16, and a dominant force in world golf throughout the 1980's, Seve's self-educated genius is not so much in the consistency of his ball-striking, but his ability to conjure shots out of thin air and seemingly *will* the ball into the hole. An inspired player, he is a magician around the green with an appetite for creating fairy-tale escape shots. He has the presence and charisma of Palmer; in every sense of the word an intimidating golfer who in the true Latin character brings fire and intensity to the golf course – as witnessed in

the Ryder Cup matches, in which Seve has proved to be such a formidable force.

When the world first caught a glimpse of the Spaniard, playing in only his second Open Championship at Royal Birkdale in 1976, Seve was an extremely long, though not always straight, hitter of the ball. His cavalier style of play was, and still is, attractive for the fact that it was utterly unpredictable, and he thrashed about the Lancashire dunes to finish alongside Jack Nicklaus in a tie for second, six behind Johnny Miller. In 1979, at Royal Lytham, he became known affectionately as the 'Car Park' champion after missing more fairways than he hit on his way to winning his first Open title.

Then just 22, Ballesteros was the youngest winner this century, and that natural affinity for links golf brought further British Open victories at St Andrews in 1984 and again at Lytham in 1988. On the latter occasion, Seve shot a final round of 65 – which he describes as the 'best of his life' – to beat Nick Price by two.

Vintage Seve – the 1984 British Open at St Andrews.

A sure putting touch and vivid imagination are the prerequisites of a US Masters champion, too, and in 1980, aged 23, Seve made history by becoming the youngest ever winner of the Masters. He triumphed there again in 1982, a victory which by general consent inspired the recent European-based domination of the green jacket, and indeed which fuelled the phenomenal growth and strength of the European Tour itself.

It is ironic that the very qualities which characterise Seve's game perhaps explain his frustration at not yet winning a US Open or US PGA title. A naturally aggressive player, the Spaniard does not speak the language of restraint which these tournaments demand. Narrow fairways and deep rough demand accuracy from the tee and a textbook strategy, while Seve plays by *feel* and intuition.

In his prime years, Seve's rather upright swing was based around a huge body turn, and his tremendous power was channelled through a fairly active hand action, which caused him not only to be erratic – particularly with the driver – but it also placed great strain on his back. Over the years these problems have cost Seve both distance and consistency, but being a true champion he has worked on a physical conditioning programme and also on improving his technique. At the time the following sequence of pictures was taken Seve was concerned specifically with shortening and flattening his swing to promote a more reliable and less strenuous action. But the magic will always be in Seve's hands.

To say aloud the words 'Seve Ballesteros' conjures up in one's mind images of a swashbuckling player; a modern-day Arnold Palmer, a man driven by a rich vein of inspiration.

The swing: *the natural grace of a born champion*

Characteristic of Seve's game is the way he so naturally sets up to the ball (**1**). Whether he's using a driver or a wedge, the club 'fits'. You can sense the beautiful softness in his hands and arms as he takes his grip and settles into position, and that softness pervades his whole body. On this matter, I like the thoughts of the great Sam

Snead, who once described the ideal grip pressure as being that which you might adopt were you to hold a small bird in your hands: not so tight that you distress the animal, but secure to the extent that it cannot escape. Wonderful imagery to have.

Over the years Seve has pondered over the early part of his swing more than any other move. He has a tendency to tilt his left shoulder down and set the

club very early, with eager wrists, and as a result his backswing is at times prone to being too steep. To get around that problem he makes a determined effort to maintain the height of his chest and left shoulder and to subdue his wrist action as he glides the clubhead away from the ball (**2, 3**).

Seve's backswing shape is now far removed from his younger days, when he had a huge shoulder turn and move off the

ball, an upright arm-plane and a hip action which tilted and twisted towards the target as he reached the top. By contrast, his swing today might not be as powerful, but this compact and flatter top of the backswing position certainly eases the strain on his back (**4**).

His upper and lower body are now more in line with one another, or as I term it, his upper body appears nicely 'stacked' on top of the lower body.

1

2

3

4

Moving into the downswing, Seve has always fought a tendency to drive with his lower body, resulting in the right arm becoming jammed in towards his side as the hands drop down into the hitting position (**5**). This leads to a narrowing of the swing arc and a dramatic steepening of the swing plane as the club approaches the ball. And this creates a problem. Good players instinctively want to avoid

swinging from the outside (i.e. 'coming over the top') and hitting shots left; to achieve that, Seve compensates by moving his head and upper body *under and back* as he swings through the ball (**6**).

Though it has improved in recent years, this distinct and characteristic 'hang-back' forces Seve to release the clubhead with an aggressive extension of the arms and hands. However, just look at the way he commits

himself to staying down on the shot (**7**) as his right side fires towards the target to a full flowing finish (**8**).

With perhaps greater natural feel than any other player, Seve has an acute awareness for the angle and position of the clubface, and such is his skill that he is able to make adjustments mid-swing, though the quality of such compensation can be variable. Seve's prowess with the mid- and

short-irons has never been in question, but in the long game his accuracy has depended mainly on the consistency of his hand action. And when his timing fails he is left fighting a tendency to hook the ball or block shots out to the right. But the sight of this glorious swing in full flight is one to behold, and it is the mark of a man who has achieved so much in the game that he continues to search for perfection.

5   6   7   8

What you can learn from Seve Ballesteros' swing

LESSON ONE: 'SOFT' ARMS LEAVE YOUR BODY RELAXED

The first thing that strikes me watching Seve set-up to a ball is how relaxed his arms are. Like a big cat ready to pounce on its prey, there is no tension in his arms, no tension in his body, which is why his swing is so graceful and pleasing to the eye. These are enviable qualities you must ingest for the sake of your own game.

Try this drill. Take your driver, hold it to waist high, and then squeeze the grip as hard as you can. Wrap your fingers together and sense a tightening in the muscle cords running up through your forearms to your shoulders and upper body. Hold that clenched position for a couple of seconds, then relax. Totally exhale, and feel that tension drain away. Your hands, arms and shoulders should now feel *'soft'*, and when you lower the clubhead to assume your normal set up position, your whole body should be athletically poised, but free of unnecessary tension.

Keeping that tension out of the arms in the initial stages of the swing is equally important. You don't want to grab onto the club as you start back, or jerk it away. Everything must be ready to flow.

So, as you work on your game, focus on maintaining a light, sensitive grip pressure when you set up to the ball, and continue on in that theme as you *flow* the club away from the ball.

LESSON TWO: THINK 'HEAD BACK' FOR UPWARD SWEEPING MOTION

Let's now turn our attention to the noticeable head movement Seve employs through the ball. This is a compensatory factor as far as he is concerned, designed to help him achieve the desired inside approach and release the club with a full extension of the arms. But out of this we can identify a useful swing thought, one that can help you to release the clubhead more forcefully with the longer clubs, and particularly the driver.

To flight your drives with a piercing trajectory, first you must cultivate a shallow clubhead arc through impact so that you sweep the ball away with a slightly ascending blow.

Nothing hurts a tee shot more than to slide one's head forward, creating a *descending* type blow on the ball. Fall into that trap and all the energy and clubhead speed is released down and into the ground (rather than *up and through* the ball), producing a variety of poor shots.

This drill will help to ensure that you don't suffer that fate, and will improve the trajectory and consistency of your tee shots. Get a friend to hold a club firmly against the target-side of your head as you set up to a ball, then relax and make your swing. As you change direction from backswing to downswing, the presence of that club will remind you to keep your head *behind* the ball as your hands and arms accelerate the clubhead through impact. [Your friend should remove the club from your head just after contact with the ball is made.] The sensation you want to achieve is that of your chin turning backwards and slightly away from the target as you release your arms and right shoulder through. That will reward you with the desired angle of approach, better contact and greater distance.

21

FRED COUPLES

BORN: OCTOBER 3RD, 1959, SEATTLE, WASHINGTON, USA. **TURNED PRO:** 1980. **HEIGHT:** 5ft 11in (1.8m).

Rarely does a player's golf swing so accurately reflect the character of its owner. One of the game's most relaxed and easy going competitors, Fred Couples graces the tour with an unbelievably nonchalant and lazy swing, and with it he creates seemingly effortless power. In a game so often saturated in complexity, Fred prefers to keep things simple. So simple that sometimes you wonder if he is trying at all.

In all sports the boy from Seattle is a natural. A useful soccer player as a youngster, his golf developed quickly upon being introduced to the game by his father, Tom, a semi-pro baseball player. There was a nine-hole course close to home, and Fred worked the driving range for free balls. Aged 18, he shot a final round of 65 to win the Washington State Open, and knew at once he'd found his niche in life. A scholarship at the University of Houston beckoned, where Fred breezed into the golf team. In his three years at Houston, he was twice named all-American, and when he turned pro in 1980, somewhat predictably, he earned his PGA Tour card at the first attempt.

With a swing best described as home-grown, Fred seems to improve with every year that passes by. His tournament record was impressive prior to a Ryder Cup debut in 1989, with three tour wins – including the prestigious Tournament Players Championship in 1984 – but the impact of that match at The Belfry, where he missed the final green with a 9-iron in his critical singles match against Christy O'Connor Jnr, was profound.

In the aftermath of that nightmare, Fred blamed himself for his team not capturing the Ryder Cup, but his close friend Raymond Floyd, America's non-playing captain that year, made certain that in the long term Fred would benefit from his experience. Thanks mostly to Floyd, the day Fred lost his innocence would also be the day he realised his true standing as a player, and in the years since he has worked harder on his game than he ever dreamed possible. He realised that he hated to lose, resolved to be much tougher, mentally, and assumed the status of a winner.

Determined to avenge his performance at The Belfry, Fred's immediate goal was to play his way into the team for the next encounter at Kiawah Island in 1991, and having done so, with multiple wins on the US Tour, he was one of Dave Stockton's most effective weapons as America sensationally regained the Cup. Later that year he won the inaugural Johnnie Walker World Championship at Tryall, in Jamaica, and continued that form with a dazzling streak of three wins in 1992. Though reluctant to acknowledge the mantle of 'superstar', Fred Couples would become the first American golfer to top the Sony world rankings, and shortly after that his efforts culminated in his first major, The US Masters.

Fred's casual style is attractive for the fact that his mind is free of technical thoughts, while a natural affinity to low scoring makes his game exciting to watch. With deceptive ease, he has the ability to carry the ball huge distances off the tee, and peppers the pin with towering irons. His power originates in the tremendous torque he generates with his swing. In the sequences that follow you will see Fred turn his shoulders beyond 100° over a relatively small hip turn; sheer athletic power that is boosted by a supple wrist action.

Fred is afflicted with a disc problem in the lower part of his back, and the golfing public can only hope that this injury does not shorten the career of this truly talented player.

Ian Woosnam helps Fred Couples don the coveted green jacket after winning the US Masters in 1992.

In creating great torque and controlling the club with a full wrist cock, Fred Couples combines the two qualities you assume of the naturally gifted long hitter.

The swing:
free and easy power

A natural fader of the ball, the shape of Couples' swing is such that from a fairly open stance he picks the club up outside the ball-to-target line going back, then drops it back in on the way down. But even though he drops it back in with a wonderfully lazy, almost nonchalant change of direction, the clubhead works slightly across the target line through impact, which creates that cut-spin.

One thing that pictures fail to convey is the rhythm of a great player. Fred has beautiful motion: his is a *flowing* action from start to finish. This quality is there from the moment he stands to the ball – look at how relaxed he appears (**1**). There is no muscular tension in his body whatsoever, and a light sensitive grip pressure has everything to do with that. Very much in the Paul Azinger mould, Couples favours a fairly strong grip, clearly showing three knuckles on the left hand and a 'cupping' in his left wrist.

We can see also that he sets up slightly open to the line, and with his hands behind the ball, which is teed up off his left heel. This hand position promotes a sweeping delivery of the clubhead through impact – perfect for the driver.

Standing with his legs relatively straight, and allowing his arms to hang freely away from his body, gives Fred the space he needs to swing the club up and away quite abruptly (**2**) – for me the most noticeable feature in the entire movement. The triangle formed between his arms and shoulders has moved and yet the torso has barely responded. While there is perhaps a slight shifting of the weight onto the right side, there is little in the way of hip turn as he approaches halfway, and only slight evidence of rotation in the chest (**3**).

Then the coiling process really

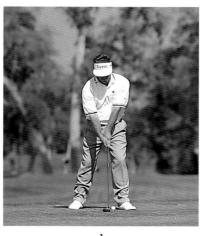

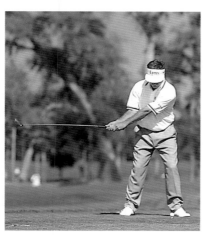

1

2

3

4

begins: Fred swings to the top with a full winding of the upper body over a relatively passive hip and leg action (**4**), which combined with a full cocking of the wrists produces a tremendous wind-up and explains his immense power.

It is interesting to note that while at the halfway stage the club appears to be swinging back on the 'outside', this huge turn enables him to whip the club up and around his body, positioning the club across the line at the top, the right elbow high and 'deep'.

An extremely supple athlete, Fred is able to achieve this very complete backswing while keeping both feet planted flat on the ground. His right leg stabilises the rotary motion of his upper body, and the big muscles in his torso are now fully 'loaded' up.

Now the key move: with a quick hip action, Fred sets off a dynamic chain reaction in which his weight moves back towards the target as the hips rotate and clear, and the right elbow drops neatly into his side (**5**). In effect he has created a 'flailing' type of action, where the club is actually *re-cocking* as he swings it back down, increasing the set angle in the wrists. The fact that his hips are fairly well open (but the shoulders closed) tells us this is an extremely powerful 'torqued' hitting position.

Fred has a very deceptive swing. Although it looks very lazy there's a tremendous amount of 'lag' stored in the downswing and terrific clubhead speed is unleashed on the ball (**6**). The right side of his body works *under* the left through impact, and he hammers the ball with his right hand. I particularly like the way Fred stays down on the shot. He releases the club with a full extension of the right arm (**7**) and, with his supple wrists, hinges the club up once again on its way to a full and flowing follow through position (**8**).

5

6

7

8

What you can learn from Fred Couples' swing

LESSON ONE: FOR MAXIMUM COIL, TURN AND STRETCH TO THE TOP

The fundamental act of turning and winding up the bigger muscles in the body – i.e. the pivot motion – is critically important to a good swing. But one of the things I see often, especially with better players, is that they actually rotate and turn their torso too early, and then *lift* their arms to reach the top of their backswing. The wonderful lesson Couples provides is that for maximum coil and power, *the later turning motion of the upper body must complete the backswing movement*.

When I study images of Fred's swing, I am struck by the fact that halfway back his shoulders have barely turned at all, yet he arrives at the top with a huge shoulder turn over a slight hip turn. This is the key to a powerful coil: you must synchronise the movement of your arms and body, as Fred does. As you work on building your swing, try to picture in your mind's eye the turning motion of your body and the swinging of the hands and arms being completed at the same time. In reality there will be a slight 'lag' effect as you reach the top – i.e. your hips will stop turning before the shoulders, the shoulders stop before the arms and the club travels further still as the weight and momentum of the clubhead stretches the muscles in your wrists and arms. That's the effect of centrifugal force.

The benefit of such a well co-ordinated backswing movement unfolds in the downswing. When you wind up your body correctly, you are all the more likely to *unwind* correctly. As you change direction, the swinging motion of your hands and arms is better synchronised with the rotation of your body coming into the ball. In other words, your arms and body *'match up'* through impact.

This is the element of *timing* we associate with a good swing – the release of the arms and clubhead harmonises with the rotary motion of the body.

LESSON TWO: CULTIVATE WRIST ACTION FOR GREATER CLUBHEAD SPEED

Fred Couples provides us with a graphic example of the way a full wrist cock multiplies the acceleration of the clubhead through impact. He 'sets' his wrists in the backswing and then retains that set angle deep into the downswing until he can no longer resist the centrifugal forces at work. His wrists then 'snap' the clubhead through at great speed before hinging up once more in the follow-through. This is a skill you must develop – remember, your wrists act as hinges in the golf swing, and they are a great source of power.

As an exercise, take a short iron, stick a tee in the end of the grip, then focus on your wrist action as you make simple half-swings, back and through. Sense that your wrists hinge up fairly vertically, so that halfway into your backswing the tee points down towards the ground. Then swing your arms down – holding the cocked position for as long as possible – and whip the clubhead through impact. Finally, check to see that your follow through mirror images your backswing – i.e. that the tee points downwards once again.

In a short space of time this drill will reward you with a sense of what a good wrist action feels like, which, when incorporated into your normal full swing will significantly increase your power potential.

JOHN DALY

BORN: APRIL 28TH, 1966, SACRAMENTO, CALIFORNIA, USA. **TURNED PRO:** 1987. **HEIGHT:** 5ft 11in (1.8m).

John Daly owes Nick Price. The 'Wild Thing' from Arkansas took centre stage when Price withdrew from the US PGA championship at Crooked Stick in 1991 to be with his wife as she delivered their first child. Driving through the night to arrive as ninth alternate, and without even so much as a warm-up round, the 25-year-old tour rookie played the starring role to win. But it was the manner in which he demolished the competition that created a folklore which will be talked about for generations to come.

The golf course at Crooked Stick, one of Pete Dye's formidable creations, might just have been built for John's all-out game. At 7,289 yards it was then the longest course ever used to stage a major championship. Heavy rain had placed a premium on the ability to carry the ball that week and with one swing thought – *'Kill'* – John made a mockery of the challenge. Averaging over 300 yards off the tee, he cut all the corners to boldly go where no man had gone before, getting home with mid- and short-irons where others were struggling with long irons and woods. For the record, he played the four par-five holes in a cumulative 12-under par.

A thoroughly natural player, John Daly not only hits the ball a long way but he plays with great feel and control around the green. He has a wonderful touch, and comparisons with a young Jack Nicklaus are by no means fanciful. But power and length aside, there is much to learn so far as managing his game is concerned. Throughout history, the great players – the players who regularly threaten in the major tournaments – are those who are versatile in their shot-making, able to fashion a game to suit all types of course and weather conditions. This is a part of the game that John needs to learn and gain experience in: he needs the discipline to channel his aggression and to play *'within'* himself. With this ability to overpower any golf course, his potential is unlimited – though potential and talent alone won't take one to the very top.

But the sheer excitement John Daly brings to the game has introduced a new dimension to world golf. Like a hurricane, his arrival came without warning and his game spells danger wherever he plays. In the 1993 US Open at Baltusrol, he became the first man to hit the 630-yard, par-5, 17th hole, in two shots, with a driver and 1-iron. John Daly's talent knows no planetary bounds, and only time will tell whether he makes the most of his God-given gift.

With his 'killer' swing, John Daly sensationally won the 1991 US PGA Championship at Crooked Stick, Indiana.

Thoroughly non-technical, John Daly's 'grip it and rip it' philosophy has caught the imagination and fuelled with excitement the world of golf.

The killer swing:
outrageous blend of strength and flexibility

John has a relatively strong left-hand grip, for which he is able to compensate with a very neutral right hand. There is a noticeable tilt across his shoulders, indicating that as he sets up to the ball he settles his weight in favour of his right side, as one should with the driver (**1**). There's also a strong straight line relationship between his left arm and the clubshaft, which gives his whole set-up a very powerful look.

Flowing his weight into his right side, John initiates the swing with a slight lateral movement of his body. Combined with a 'rolling' action of the left forearm, this lateral movement sets the clubhead travelling very low to the ground and also a long way inside the ball-to-target line (**2**). The stage is thus set for a very flat backswing plane at the halfway mark (**3**). But just take note of the great extension and the powerful coiling motion of his upper body.

John proceeds to make a *huge* turn with his upper body, while the arms can be seen to lift the club onto a more upright plane, and the right elbow moves away to a very high position at the top (reminiscent of a young Jack Nicklaus). All of which culminates in probably the most talked about feature of John's swing – how far back he takes the club (**4**).

With the majority of top players, the coiling effect is maximised when the club is approximately in a parallel position at the top, but John maximises his torque with a swing that goes way beyond parallel and creates a huge wide arc. Such an overswing is not a problem if the big muscles continue winding all the way to the top. It's only a fault if the coil stops early, the swing arc

1

2

3

4

collapses, or grip pressure is lost. None of that for John. His long swing is simply the result of a huge turn, the lifting of his arms from halfway back, plus a very full wrist cock. And on top of all that John is extremely supple.

It is in the change of direction, though, that this tremendous power is channelled. In easing his lower body towards the target – a subtle movement in the left knee and left hip – John *eases* his weight back on to his left side

and achieves the classic 'squat' position, in the mould of Sam Snead (**5**). A great transitional move. The legs are braced, the hips are turning back to the left, and the power is being stored ready for release as the right arm works in towards his side.

Just look at his clubhead lag and the angle between his wrist and the club shaft as he swings down to the ball (**6**) – wow! From here, there's a distinct clearing of the left side as the clubhead is

unleashed at the ball – a great impact position where the left arm and shaft form a straight line (**7**). I like the way John stays down so well on the ball, and we can see that his whole left side has firmed up to receive the hit.

This firmness in his left side is ultimately what allows his right side to explode through the ball as is depicted in John's trademark finish (**8**) – his right shoulder all the way through to the target and the club wrapped around his back.

Again, this final position shows John's immense flexibility and the amount of clubhead speed imparted.

You can just sense the power in this swing – it seems to jump off the page. The torque, the wind up, the leverage – whatever else you want to attach to power – it's all here. Nobody in the modern game hits the ball with the clubhead speed John Daly is able to generate, and yet he maintains perfect balance throughout.

5

6

7

8

What you can learn from John Daly's swing

**BUILD POWER, STORE IT,
AND THEN RELEASE IT**

This is not a swing I would recommend for mere mortals. Unless you are very strong and flexible it's virtually impossible – and foolish – to attempt to swing the way John Daly does. But there are a number of things you can learn from his powerful action, not least the principle of *retaining* the power and *releasing* it at the right point on the downswing.

I believe it's important for every player to establish his or her maximum coil position – i.e. the point at which your back is fully turned on the target and your upper body is wound to its fullest extent. In John's case that coiling effect and power is maximised with the club way beyond parallel, and such is his suppleness that the left heel barely lifts off the ground. [As far as the issue of lifting the left heel is concerned, you may have to raise it somewhat to maximise your coil – particularly if you suffer from a lack of flexibility. Just be sure to lift it *late* in the backswing.]

Take a driver, and focus on building coil as you make your

backswing. Sense resistance in your knees and thighs and wind your upper body smoothly to its fullest extent. Turn your back on the target and swing the club at least to the parallel – maximise that coil to the *nth* degree. Then, having built up all that energy, focus on *retaining* it as you make the transition and your swing changes direction. This is what John does so well.

To do this, you want to feel a distinct *sitting down* in your lower body as your weight starts to move gradually towards the target. Make this a passive change of direction: sense a split in your knees as the left knee pulls away from the right. Think about sticking your rear out behind you. This key assists in *maintaining the resistance in your lower body*, and keeps the legs anchored. In your swing, don't think of making a *backswing* or a *downswing*. Think more along the lines of your backswing and downswing blending into one fluid motion. It is important that you make this distinction. Not only does it help you to establish a good rhythm, but it enables you to achieve that powerful sit-down *squat* position as the arms swing down, whereupon you can release and accelerate the club through impact and hit against a firm left side.

One way to appreciate the sensation of hitting against or *into* a firm left side and fully release that stored power is to try this drill. Turn your left foot in a few degrees at address, as you see in the accompanying illustration. With your foot in such a position, your left leg automatically firms up to provide resistance in the impact area, while your hips clear at tremendous rate, enabling you to snap the clubhead through at full speed. The clearance of the hips with the left leg solid (as opposed to a weak sliding motion that many golfers employ) might not get you hitting it as far as Mr Daly, but it should certainly reward you with a few more precious yards.

LAURA DAVIES

BORN: OCTOBER 5TH, 1963, COVENTRY, ENGLAND. **TURNED PRO:** 1985. **HEIGHT:** 5ft 10in (1.8m).

The traditional 'locker-room' image of lady professionals not hitting the ball a particularly long way, but hitting it pretty straight, are blown right out of the window when you witness the phenomenal power of Britain's Laura Davies. Not only is she by a wide margin the 'longest' player ever to grace the women's game, she could give many of her counterparts on the men's tour a 20-yard start.

Often referred to as the 'John Daly of women's golf' – and both claim never to have had a formal lesson – Laura took up golf at the age of fourteen, and her first handicap was 26; six years later it was plus-5. She turned professional in 1985, at the age of 22, and topped the European Order of Merit in her debut year. In 1986 she duplicated that feat, her four wins in Europe including the Women's British Open, which she won at Royal Birkdale. But it was in 1987 that she struck gold with an awesome display of controlled power golf to win the US Women's Open, after a play-off with America's Joanne Carner and Japan's superstar, Ayako Okamoto.

A natural talent, Laura's style of golf typifies the way she lives her life – go for broke, no holding back, and take a gamble at every opportunity. She is a free spirit who does not care to focus on the technical aspects of the swing, and one who can happily put her clubs away for a month, then come out on tour refreshed and play peerless golf. That she proved in Australia, winning the Queensland Open in 1993 without once visiting the range. Her confident, cavalier style was the catalyst so desperately important to the growth of the Women's European Tour. Reminiscent of a young Seve Ballesteros, not only do her solo exploits around the world reflect well on her home circuit, but her tenacious spirit inspired the European team to an historic victory in the Solheim Cup at Dalmahoy in 1992.

There is no doubt that Laura Davies is the longest hitter of the ball in the women's game, a talent that makes her a drawing card wherever she plays. Much less talked about is her natural ability to invent three-quarter shots, choking down on the club to manufacture what her mind sees –

Victory celebration at the end of the 1994 McDonald's LPGA Championship at DuPont Country Club, Wilmington, Delaware.

a versatility that has been amply rewarded. In 1994, with the most dazzling run of form since Nancy Lopez won nine events in 1979, Laura became the first player – male or female – to win on five different tours in a season. In successive weeks she triumphed twice in Europe, won her second major – the LPGA Championship – and with further victories in Australia, Japan and the Philippines, became the first women ever to win more than $1m in a single year, and the first European player to top the LPGA Order of Merit.

Not bad for a girl who loathes to practise.

*Never before
has a player
dominated the
women's game
with such an
overwhelming
display of power
as the self-taught
Laura Davies.*

The swing:
upper body dominant

There are some pretty unorthodox moves here, but Laura is a smart player: she takes care of the fundamentals, and the fundamentals take care of her. With a good grip and set-up position, she gives herself the opportunity to hit a good shot *every time* she steps up to the ball. That's lesson number one.

Generally a left-to-right player, Laura assumes a tall, athletic posture, her hands positioned ahead of the ball, which for the driver is teed opposite the inside of her left heel (**1**). It's interesting to note how squarely her feet are positioned at address: she settles a higher percentage of her weight on her right side, and positions her head well behind the ball. The left arm and the clubshaft form a straight line, and her right arm

and right shoulder sit considerably lower than the left.

There is clearly good balance here. The lower body is poised to support the powerful turning of the upper body, which defines Laura's action. As she moves the club away from the ball (**2**), the backswing is set underway with a characteristic leaning of the upper body away from the target. Notice there is very little turning motion at this point: the hands and arms

move quite independently in the early stages of the swing, while the lower body remains passive – much in the style of Fred Couples.

After that initial moveaway, Laura rolls the club on a fairly flat plane (**3**), but from here the turning motion of her body and the upward swinging action of the left arm put the club in a great position at the top (**4**). For a strong girl she is also extremely supple. Look at how far she has

1

2

3

4

turned her left shoulder under her chin, and the superb coil she has created as the lower body has resisted the winding of the upper body.

The key to Laura's power is in her change of direction. As her left side begins to unwind, note the subtle movement of the left knee, left hip and left shoulder as each in turn pulls away from its opposite number (**5**). From the top of the swing we can also see that

the hands have moved down quite a few inches relative to the short distance the clubhead has travelled. This shows there is tremendous stress on the shaft, and an unbelievable amount of 'lag' on the clubhead as the hands work down towards impact (**6**). As her left side straightens to support the hit, there is then a tremendous unleashing of the clubhead (**7**) as Laura smashes through the ball to a very full finish.

Study how well she delivers the clubhead: halfway down, as the club approaches the ball it is bang on plane, the shaft angle clearly matching that of her right forearm. Although her hands are a long way from her body at impact, notice also how closely her left arm and shaft resemble her original set-up position.

Another interesting feature of this swing is the behaviour of the left heel. From a position which

looks fairly orthodox at the top of the backswing, the foot squares itself off as the left side pulls away from the right, and the sheer speed and thrust of her downswing causes her left heel to be forced up off the ground through impact. Laura may appear to be off balance, but her strong legs are able to help her stay down through the shot – and just look at how balanced she arrives at the finish (**8**).

5

6

7

8

What you can learn from Laura Davies' swing

LEFT SHOULDER LEADS AND DOMINATES THE DOWNSWING

Perhaps the most valuable lesson Laura gives us is in the way she unwinds the left side of her body from the top of the backswing. Effectively signalling the change of direction, her left shoulder separates and pulls away from her chin, and this is a key leverage point and power-move for any golfer to follow.

Having coiled behind the ball, the problem for many players is knowing how to release the spring; how do you initiate the correct downswing sequence and get the left side of the body moving back towards the target?

A useful key is to focus on the movement of your left shoulder – sense that it pulls away from the chin as your upper body moves laterally towards the target, while your knees and hips remain solid. Once you achieve that feeling of separation, your left arm will be free to pull the club down towards the hitting area, and you will naturally retain the angle in your wrists, so important for solid ball striking.

The following exercises will help you. First, take a club in your left hand, and choke down a little on the grip (as you see on the opposite page). Then grab your left wrist with your right hand and make your backswing. Turn your left shoulder under your chin, and hold that position momentarily. Now, as you unwind, sense that the whole left side of your body leads the movement forward: with your legs braced, feel your left shoulder pull away from your chin as you unwind towards the target.

As you rehearse this power move, hold on to the angle between your left wrist and the clubshaft for as long as you can before accelerating the clubhead through impact. Pull the club down to a point where the clubhead is 'lagging' behind your hands – a torqued position all good ball-strikers seek to achieve – and then let the speed of the release free-wheel your arms and body to a full finish.

The second exercise is a dynamic isometric move, and it works like this. Grab hold of the 'lat' muscles beneath your left shoulder with your right hand – as illustrated above – and rehearse your backswing movement. Then, as you begin to

unwind towards the target with the left side of your body, pull in the opposite direction with your right hand. Hold this two-directional transitional move for a few seconds, and repeat the exercise several times. Very soon you will appreciate the athletic way in which your left side initiates the forward movement, which with regular practice will enable you to create tremendous re-coil speed as you explode through the ball.

ERNIE ELS

BORN: OCTOBER 17TH, 1969, JOHANNESBURG, SOUTH AFRICA. **TURNED PRO:** 1989. **HEIGHT:** 6ft 3in (1.9m).

Had the mood taken him, Ernie Els might have become one of South Africa's most formidable tennis players. At the age of 14, he was Eastern Transvaal's senior champion. On another day, he might have chosen cricket. Or perhaps rugby. He had a power and a perfection rarely found in one so young. The choice was his alone.

Ernie decided he liked golf, and ever since has set the world on fire with such a display of raw talent, nerve and touch that nobody dare predict just how far he might go. His record prior to his victory in the US Open at Oakmont in 1994 was quite phenomenal. He won the World Junior championship in San Diego at the age of 15, already a scratch player, beating among others Phil Mickelson in to second place. At 16, he was the youngest-ever winner of the South African Amateur. Then, having turned professional in 1989, he won the big three tournaments of the South African tour – the Open, the PGA and the Masters – before embarking on a career in Europe.

Perhaps more impressive – and certainly more telling – is his record in the Majors, and particularly the British Open. He was fifth at Muirfield in 1992, and sixth at Royal St George's (Sandwich) in 1993, where he broke 70 in all four rounds, a record matched only by Greg Norman, who shot the lowest ever final round – 64 – to win that year. Later in 1994, Ernie added the World Matchplay title to his US Open crown and ran away with the inaugural Sarazen World Open championship. Players normally achieve this sort of maturity in their thirties; Ernie is

Holding aloft the 1994 US Open trophy.

way ahead of his time.

Standing 6ft 3in out of his spikes, Ernie Els has the build of a durable modern champion. He is broad across the shoulders and has strong legs and forearms. But he is also extremely supple, and swings the club with great elegance for such a big man. Indeed, his tempo could be his greatest asset – Gary Player compares Ernie with Sam Snead – and his languid mood certainly enables him to repeat a golf swing that is full of simplicity. His thought process is 'feel' oriented, with the focus on matching his arm swing and body turn in

A typical Els' power-drive during the 1994 US Open at Oakmont, Pennsylvania.

order that he can take advantage of the tremendous leverage in his swing. Too many swing thoughts only confuse him – as they will you.

In common with other power players who seem to swing within themselves, Ernie has also been blessed with the ability to call on an extra 20 or 30 yards at any given time, a terrific advantage. He is strong, and he knows how to exercise tremendous hand speed within the framework of a controlled body action. If he wants to hit the ball further, he simply slows his swing and builds an even greater coil – as Jack Nicklaus did in his prime. A slow wind up, followed by a lazy change of direction, enables him to accelerate like the wind and rip through the ball. A cool, calm, confident customer, Ernie Els looks certain to be one of the true *bona fide* stars of the next century.

In every generation of golfers one or two stand out from the crowd. By winning the US Open at just 24 years of age, there is no question that Ernie Els is something very special.

The swing: *flowing tempo of a natural athlete*

Here, with a 2-iron, Ernie looks poised to make a good swing. He has spent a lot of time working on the shape and structure of his address position, and for a tall man has what I term a beautifully 'natural' set-up – the pictures suggest he is relaxed, but in a strong, athletic sense (**1**).

Ernie works hard on good balance and alignment. Note how well his feet, knees, hips, shoulders and eyes all run parallel to one another – as most players should try to achieve. His arms just seem to hang from the shoulders, the lower part of his back is straight, and the head tilted slightly behind the ball. I like the gap between his knees, too. They are not 'pinched' in, and his feet are about shoulder-width apart. All positive factors in assisting a good

turn behind the ball, particularly with the longer clubs.

Ernie moves the club, his arms and chest away 'together', and he keeps the clubhead well outside his hands (**2**). There is a tremendous resistance in his lower body as the arms swing back, and as the wrists hinge and the right elbow folds, Ernie sets the club on a plane that is slightly steeper than the original shaft angle made at address (**3**), which I like, particularly for tall

players. Halfway back the butt-end of the club points down between his feet and the ball. That's a useful check to make.

With a solid knee action, Ernie swings his left arm across his chest to arrive in a compact position at the top, in which his right elbow is well 'tucked' for a tall man, and the swing on an excellent plane (**4**). Ernie exhibits great flexibility here as he fully winds up his upper body with relatively little

1   2   3   4

hip turn. He appears to be like a stretched elastic band, ready to snap forward. Ernie's suppleness enables him to keep a very steady head with the left foot firmly on the ground and left arm straight. Study this position at the top – it really is a picture full of information.

As he changes direction, Ernie now exerts his immense power. His body is essentially passive as he begins to unwind, especially the upper body. The lower body initiates the downswing, but there is no rush or excessive 'drive' as the knees and hips move towards the target (**5**).

This is an area of the swing he has really improved on. As the left side of his body starts to unwind, the right side holds momentarily, as witnessed by the fact his right foot remains flat on the ground. This passive unwinding of his lower body has allowed his arms to fall into place, while retaining his fantastic arc width and increasing his wrist cocks – no wonder he hits the ball so far. His head is steady, eyes are fixed on the ball, and the left shoulder has moved well away from his chin. It's now a case of waiting for the moment to fire and releasing all that energy with his right side through impact.

The key point here is that his arm speed and body turn are perfectly matched, and he plants the clubface squarely on the back of the ball (**6**). His weight moves across into his left side, the head is steady behind the ball and the arms are fully extended. There is no holding back. With this full-flowing, unrestricted release (**7**), Ernie wraps the clubshaft around the back of his head. Beautiful. The right shoulder points at the target and his hips have cleared all the way through (**8**). A classic portrait of grace and power.

5   6   7   8

What you can learn from Ernie Els' swing

LESSON ONE: INCREASE 'LEVERAGE' AS YOU CHANGE DIRECTION

In days gone by, pro's would love to be paired with the great Sam Snead for the simple reason his legendary rhythm was contagious. The same is true of Ernie Els today: his swing just seems to gather speed all the way to the finish. For me, one of the key areas of this gathering pace is his change of direction; the way Ernie manages to maintain and even increase the torque factor as he throws the gears into reverse.

This is a critical area to work on. A good golf swing is not composed of a backswing and downswing, though that is how most golfers tend to think about it. It is in fact a blended, *continuous motion.* Something is always moving and flowing, which creates rhythm and momentum. Some of the most destructive faults known in golf occur here in the transition period – *'casting'* the clubhead, *'hitting from the top'*, *'jerking'* the

club down, and so on. Ugly phrases which describe ugly swings.

The key to a fluid motion is to unwind from the ground up. It is not a case of just pulling the club down. Too many people think that way, and as a result lose all their power before getting to the

ball. A good key thought is to unwind the lower body and *resist* with your upper body, as Ernie does. This enables gravity to pull the arms down smoothly and unhurriedly – all the speed being saved until the last possible moment. Watch as he changes direction: his lower body rotates

back towards the target while his upper body is still relatively closed to the target line – i.e. aiming to the right. The relative position of his hips (open) and his shoulders (closed) creates a tremendous leverage, which then boosts the speed of his arms.

A simple drill will help you

appreciate this sensation. Hook a club through your elbows behind your back, as illustrated, and rehearse your pivot motion. Focus on the movement forward: work on the feeling of the hips being open, the shoulders closed as you change direction and ease into your downswing. Feel your left knee move slightly forward and your left hip rotate, and at the same time keep your chest turned away from the target.

Hold this position for a few seconds – you should be aware of a tightness across your back, in your stomach, and pressure in your legs. This reflects the resistance and torque present between the upper and lower body.

If you can develop this synchronised unwinding of the body in the swing itself your arms will fall naturally into the hitting position, and then it's a case of the upper body trying to catch up with the lower body as you rotate and accelerate through impact. And the more you can exaggerate that feeling of 'stretch' at the start of the downswing, the more leverage and clubhead speed you will unleash through the ball.

LESSON TWO: UNWIND TO A FULL FINISH – AND *HOLD IT*

One of the most valuable lessons we learn from Ernie Els is also one of the most obvious: the poise, balance and weight transfer he exhibits at the finish. This is a fundamental element of every good swing, and a useful thought is simply '*swing to the finish*'. If you can achieve that you instinctively get away from any tendency to hit *at* the ball (which can inhibit your release) and instead round off your swing with a classically poised position, your body relatively straight, head back just a touch, belt buckle facing the target and weight solidly into the left side.

To encourage this, imagine that the ball simply gets in the way of a good swing – that focuses your attention on swinging *through* the shot, and not 'at' the ball. As you arrive at the finish, virtually all

of your weight should be supported on your left side, your right shoulder should be pointing at the target, your knees touching, left foot flat, right foot up on the toe.

Now put your follow-through position to the test: as you swing to the finish, you should be able

to lift your right foot up off the ground momentarily. Ernie achieves all this and more, with his hands comfortably positioned behind his neck and the club across his shoulders – a position you should try to imitate.

NICK FALDO

BORN: JULY 18TH, 1957, WELWYN GARDEN CITY, ENGLAND. **TURNED PRO:** 1976. **HEIGHT:** 6ft 3in (1.9m)

In 1984, I met Nick Faldo for the first time in Sun City, where he was playing in the Million Dollar Challenge. I knew his game had for a while been erratic, and on Nick Price's suggestion he asked me to take a look at his swing. Faldo told me there and then he wanted to change his technique in order that he might flight the ball more consistently and shape shots to order. He needed to do this, he felt, if he was going to achieve his goal of winning the British Open.

I learned very quickly that Nick Faldo had always believed in being the best he could possibly be. Here was a man who in 1983 had the lowest scoring average in the world, who won five times in Europe and topped the Order of Merit there. Not good enough. Faldo was determined to work until he made himself into the best golfer in the world. I have never met – and nor can I imagine – a more focused professional.

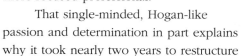

Major man – the 1992 British Open at Muirfield, Scotland.

That single-minded, Hogan-like passion and determination in part explains why it took nearly two years to restructure his swing. Nick wasn't satisfied with it only being partially right; in no aspect of his life does he deal in half measures. He wanted to build a swing that would repeat; a swing that would enable him to manipulate the flight of the ball; a swing he could rely on under the most intense heat golf could offer: *Major* pressure. This meant a lot of hard work and the acceptance that his game would get worse before it got better – in the darkest days he slipped to 42nd on the European money list.

Though it had been successful, Faldo's old swing was very much a throwback to the 1970's style of teaching which emphasised the very wide, one-piece takeaway, high hands at the top of the backswing, and 'driving' the legs in the downswing. Great natural rhythm, a red-hot putting stroke and permanent residence on the practice tee made him a winner. But standing 6ft 3in tall, Nick was basically a 'handsy' player, with an alarming lateral slide in his swing and a tendency to get steep on the ball. If I might condense two year's work into a brief sentence, his sheer determination to raise his game enabled him to re-assess his fundamentals, shallow the plane of his swing and entrust the bigger muscles in the body to control the path of the clubhead.

In 1987, with the wraps taken off a solid and efficient 'body-controlled' swing, Faldo silenced his critics with 18 consecutive pars in trying conditions to win his first major championship – the British Open at Muirfield. Two years later he won his first US Masters' title in a play-off with Scott Hoch, and in 1990 became one of only four players to defend the green jacket when he defeated Raymond Floyd, again in a play-off. Driven with intense mental energy, he won majors four and five with victory in the British Open at St Andrews in 1990, and again at Muirfield in 1992.

Nick thrives on the major championships and gears his schedule around them, the ultimate goal being to win all four in a single year – the Grand Slam – which he believes he can do. By no means an exceptionally long hitter, his game is built on precision, and while modern equipment may, to some degree, be responsible for neutralising spin, Nick remains one of the few players in the world truly able to *work* the ball. In golf there is always a trade-off. With Nick his artistry to shape shots to his imagination makes up for his supposed lack of distance off the tee. In the final analysis, I very much doubt he'd trade his pinpoint control and accuracy for a handful of yards.

The incredible determination and belief of Nick Faldo makes him a role model to golfers of all ages around the world in terms of the rewards practice and hard work can bring.

The swing: *arms and body in perfect harmony*

Nick applies the same smooth tempo with all his clubs, and being a great iron player it's amazing how many of his shots finish pin high. Nick is a very straight hitter of the ball, and does not impart much side spin unless the shot calls for it. He's a *swinger* of the golf club, as opposed to a 'hitter'.

At 6ft 3in tall, with long limbs, Nick is forced to think hard about his balance and tempo – it's all too easy to get arms and body out of 'sync'. When Nick has a problem it stems from his set-up and over-use of his hips and legs – tendencies he will have to contend with to some degree for the rest of his career.

A perfect example of a neutral grip in a finely balanced set-up, Nick attaches great importance to creating a good foundation for his swing. As we can see his body is square to the target line, his legs acting as a solid platform for his upper body, the lower back straight and the arms hanging in an extended neutral position (**1**).

Priming the swing, he waggles the clubhead to free his arms and shoulders of any tension, and with the key thought 'rotate and set', he moves the club, his arms and chest away in perfect harmony (**2**).

'Rotate and set' – that simple phrase reminds Nick to rotate his left forearm across his chest and hinge his wrists up to set the club on plane. Maintaining the flex in his right knee, Nick works on the principle that his wrists should be fully hinged (and the club set on the correct plane) by the time his swing is about halfway back (**3**). Once he has the club in this position, it's hard to imagine Nick ever making a poor swing, as from then on he eliminates any wasted hand and arm motion

1   2   3   4

as his body assumes control. The big muscles in the upper torso complete their wind up, placing the club in a beautiful slot at the top (**4**), with the shaft slightly short of the horizontal. Note how the angle of the clubface and the left forearm are parallel to one another. Textbook stuff.

Now for Nick's speciality: unwinding his upper body over a stabilised lower body, see how easily he drops the club onto a shallow downswing plane – the

right arm straightens slightly, and the shaft bisects the right elbow, which is exactly the checkpoint he uses (**5**). A perfect position from which to deliver the clubhead through impact.

As the club meets the ball, the legs are stabilising the swing, which allows Nick to time his release perfectly (**6**). The clubshaft and left arm form a straight line at impact, and the upper part of his left arm remains close to his chest as he maintains

the spine angle established at address. This explains why Nick's ball-striking is so consistent.

Once again, there's no wasted hand and arm motion whatsoever in this action. His body, which you will notice is open to the target line at impact, is very much controlling the show, and looking down the line, note how the angle of the shaft is virtually identical to the position it held at address. Perfect for great iron play.

This distinct body-controlled release is exactly what Nick has worked for. His swing is an ideal example of how the big muscles in the torso control the small muscles in the hands and arms. Nick's key thoughts through impact and beyond are to get his chest rotating aggressively through towards the target (**7**) and to finish with his hands well left of his body. A classic ending to a classic swing (**8**).

5

6

7

8

What you can learn from Nick Faldo's swing

LESSON ONE: FOCUS ON THE ROTATION OF YOUR LEFT FOREARM

Symptomatic of Nick Faldo's swing in the early 1980s was a tendency for his arms and body to work independently of one another through impact. Now, after many years of hard work and constant re-assessment, his athletic swing features a much more co-ordinated and reliable blending of arm-swing and body turn – a whole new ball game.

For Nick, one of the most important lessons was simply to focus on the gentle rotation of his left forearm away from the ball. That brought an immediate benefit: first, he found that he automatically shallowed the plane of his swing, and encouraged his arms to swing more *around* his body. Second, in using his left arm correctly he gradually levelled the plane of his shoulder turn to the point where he was able to fire his right side through the ball without fear of hooking. The same swing thoughts could help your game.

As a drill, place a glove under your left armpit, and try to keep it there as you make *half swings* with a short iron. Feel the link between your left arm and your chest as you gently rotate your left forearm back and through: make that a gradual rotation clockwise in the backswing and counter-clockwise through the ball.

Through impact, you should sense that your left arm and the clubshaft form a straight line. When you revert back to a full swing without the glove you will appreciate the consistency of a body-controlled release.

LESSON TWO: CONTROL TRAJECTORY WITH YOUR CHEST

A simple way to hit high and low shots is to focus on the position of your chest bone – or your shirt buttons – at the point of contact. The relative position of your sternum to that of the ball at the moment of impact influences greatly the trajectory and shape of your shots. Experiment with these ideas on the practice tee to improve your shotmaking in the fashion of Nick Faldo.

To hit a low shot, sense that you rotate your upper body through impact so your shirt buttons are trying to get in line with the ball, your shoulders relatively level and the club travelling parallel to the ground through impact. This body-dominated release is often referred to as *'covering the ball'*. Your body weight will be a little more into the left side at impact, producing a low-flighted shot.

Conversely, to hit a higher flying shot, the ball should be positioned a little further forward in the stance, and your focus this time should be on releasing the club more with your hands and arms, positioning your shirt buttons further back at the point of contact. This positions your right shoulder a little lower than the left, and produces a more ascending angle of approach and a higher, softer trajectory.

RAYMOND FLOYD

BORN: SEPTEMBER 4TH, 1942, FORT BRAGG, NORTH CAROLINA, USA. **TURNED PRO:** 1961. **HEIGHT:** 6ft 1in (1.8m).

One word sums up Raymond Floyd: determination. Anyone who witnessed his victory in the US Open at Shinnecock Hills in 1986 will remember forever those steely eyes, as the man they call the 'Stare Master' lost himself in a single-minded cocoon of concentration to shoot a last round 66, and become at 43, for four years at least, the oldest winner in the tournament's history. At 45, Hale Irwin, succeeded Raymond to that honour at Medinah in 1990.

As a youngster growing up in North Carolina, golf and baseball fought hard for Floyd's affection. His father was the pro at Fort Bragg, where the formal coaching extended only to the fundamentals, which Raymond used to develop his own unique style of planting the clubhead squarely on the back of the ball. His talent for sports was soon to be recognised, and having won the Jaycees Junior championship, aged 17, he found himself in a dilemma: with pen in hand, he was poised over a contract to join the Cleveland Indians as a professional baseball player. But in his heart he knew he always wanted to be a golf pro.

A well-built man, with powerful legs and a solid, stocky frame, Floyd is by no means a technical player. In his formative years as a pro he learned by watching and taking notice of what the great players of that era had to say – Arnold Palmer and Ben Hogan, particularly, and while his swing may not fit the classical mould it certainly repeats. When in 1963 he won the St Petersburg Open at the age of 20, he became the tour's youngest winner since Horton Smith in 1928. In 1992, aged 50, he became the first player to win on the regular

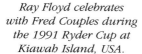

Ray Floyd celebrates with Fred Couples during the 1991 Ryder Cup at Kiawah Island, USA.

and senior US tours in the same season. A tribute to the resilience of his grinding golf, tied to a wonderfully imaginative short game, Floyd's career has successfully spanned four decades.

Above all else, Raymond Floyd is a cunning manager of his game. He has always enjoyed the ability to work the ball, and his control of distance – particularly with the short irons – has made him especially dangerous at Augusta. Always a gutsy front runner, Floyd won the US Masters in 1976 at his 12th attempt, when he lead from start to finish with rounds of 65-66-70-70 to win by eight shots. An example of his smart thinking was leaving the 1-iron out of the bag, and using instead a 5-wood, with which he could flight high balls to hold the hard greens on the long holes. It worked. Floyd was 13 under par for the sixteen times he played Augusta's four par-5's, and his aggregate of 271 tied Nicklaus' record score of 1970.

Raymond won his first major, the US PGA Championship in 1969, and earned Ryder Cup honours that same year. The team event remains his favourite in golf and he was non-playing captain at The Belfry in 1989. Two years later, Dave Stockton selected him as a wild-card for the 1991 matches at Kiawah Island. There, the oldest player on either team, Floyd produced some inspired golf to defeat Jose Maria Olazabal and help the USA reclaim the cup. As Payne Stewart once said of Floyd's intense concentration: 'His eyes seem to be staring at something you can't see'.

Floyd brought that stare to the Doral Ryder Open in 1992, where just 18 days after his Miami home had been burnt nearly to the ground, he employed his vast powers of concentration to clean the field and match Sam Snead's record of winning PGA tour events in four decades. Such is the metal and determination of the man.

*The desire to win is what separates champions from ordinary folk, and with over twenty
tour wins, including four Majors, Raymond Floyd is the ultimate bare-knuckle fighter.*

The swing:

a commercial success

You could describe Raymond's swing as individualistic – one designed around his body type: stocky with short arms. His swing repeats – certainly – and he has great rhythm. And while the pictures deny you the opportunity to appreciate this, shuffling about on his feet and waggling the club as he sets up to make his swing is his way of staying loose; it helps him make a smooth moveaway from the ball. His key is to keep in *motion*.

Floyd's swing may appear unorthodox, but from a technical standpoint, only the backswing raises comment – the downswing is great. Moving from a set-up position where his arms are fully extended away from his body (**1**), the oddity is in the way his wrists roll and fan the clubhead severely away from the ball on a flat plane, which is particularly noticeable from the rear (**2**). In order to recover the•path of his swing, there is then a distinct 'lifting' of the arms (**3**) as he swings to the top, where the wrists arrive fully cocked (**4**).

For a man of his build, he has a big turn away with the right side of his body. In Raymond's case, the angle of his right foot out at address, combined with a locked right leg and active left heel, aids his turning motion.

The down-the-line view will reveal Floyd's magic move. Look at the way the right elbow floats free of his upper body at the top, a most distinctive characteristic. Jack Nicklaus – who was of a similar build in his younger days – was also known for his 'flying' right elbow, which although is not recommended from a strictly technical perspective enables the

1

2

3

4

player who is bulky across the chest to swing his arms up and maximise the radius of his backswing.

As he changes direction, his legs squat and brace, and the floating right arm now drops down towards the area of his right hip, immediately placing the club on an excellent plane as it tracks the ball (**5**). Floyd has always played from a fairly upright backswing position, but that great first move down, where the plane shallows just perfectly, is his whole key. The clubshaft matching the angle of his right forearm is ideal (**6**). Now, exhibiting great strength, he retains the angle in his wrists deep into the hitting area, whereupon he can release his right side through the ball.

For a big man, with broad shoulders and big hips, there is very little wasted motion here. The hands play very little part in the swing (a fade is his bread-and-butter shot), and while Floyd might not rotate his body as aggressively as some through the ball, he does create a great deal of clubhead speed with the unwinding of his right side and the release of his right arm. With a steady head, he hits aggressively into a tall, firm left side (**7**) as his right shoulder fires under his chin and towards the target. This explains why he is such a good fairway wood and long iron player.

Here is an example of a man who stays very well *behind* the ball, delivering a good sweeping motion and swinging to a balanced finish (**8**). This just goes to show that while a perfect backswing may help, the real quality of the shot is dependent on how good the downswing is.

5

6

7

8

What you can learn from Raymond Floyd's swing

TRAIN YOUR RIGHT ARM – THROW A BALL, DROP THE GLOVE

If you are broad across the chest, don't ever attempt to tuck your right elbow into the side of your body on the backswing. If you make an effort to keep your right arm and elbow too 'connected' with your body, you end up with a restricted, narrow backswing position, one without the necessary leverage to generate any significant clubhead speed in the downswing.

Floyd is the perfect example to demonstrate how the arms must have freedom to swing the club down on the correct plane and path. Look back at the position he achieves at the top: the right elbow is 'floating' away from the body, and then, on the downswing, moves into a great delivery position – on plane with plenty of width. The following two drills will help you to train the proper right arm action:

(*1*) Take a golf ball and rehearse a side-arm throwing motion – go for maximum distance. Wind up as fully as you can, and feel the way your right arm instinctively works out and away from your body as you draw your hand back. Then, as you move forward to throw the ball at the target, encourage your right elbow to work down on a shallow plane – i.e. one that sends it in towards the side of your body as it approaches the release point, as you see in the illustration. In so doing you will create a powerful 'flailing' type of action with your elbow and wrist that catapults the throw and extends the right arm and the ball out towards the target.

A similar 'throwing' sensation should then be felt with a club in your hands as you make a normal swing. Focus on the following: first, *right elbow away from the body on the backswing*, then, *right elbow close to the body on the downswing*, and finally, *fully release and straighten the right arm through impact.*

(*2*) Another way to obtain this feeling of a floating right elbow on the backswing is to place a glove under your right armpit, and then address a ball. As you then approach the top of your backswing, raise your right elbow somewhat and allow the glove to fall free (right). Return the elbow to your side as you then change direction and release the club. Simple, but effective.

The importance of the right arm action in the swing has, in my opinion, been very much underestimated. Working on it can really help the width and plane of your swing. It helps to create more 'lag', improves one's release and ultimately helps you achieve the twin goals of distance and direction. You solidly built golfers should give these drills a try.

DAVID FROST

BORN: SEPTEMBER 11TH, 1959, CAPE TOWN, SOUTH AFRICA. **TURNED PRO:** 1981. **HEIGHT:** 5ft 11in (1.8m).

In the eyes of his peers, David Frost has one of the most desirable golf swings in the world today. Compact and technically simple to repeat, it is a swing that has won its owner several million dollars and a reputation as a resolutely determined player who is capable of winning at the highest level. A play-off victory over Ben Crenshaw to capture the 1989 NEC World Series of Golf (and with it a 10-year exemption to play the PGA Tour), and back-to-back wins in the Sun City Million Dollar Challenge (1989-1990), proves David's ability to play well under pressure, but at the time of writing he has yet to break in to the ranks of the major league.

David Frost collects the winning cheque at the Million Dollar Golf Challenge in Sun City, South Africa in 1990 .

Like his swing, David's progression in the game has been slow and methodical. Growing up in the comfort of a 300-acre wine grape and peach farm on the fringes of Cape Town in South Africa, he took his interest in golf from his father, who played at the Stellenbosch Golf Club, 30 miles from town. As a teenager David enjoyed playing many sports – particularly rugby – but he concentrated on golf from the age of 17. By 21 he was one of South Africa's leading amateur players and had represented his country three times.

Upon turning professional in 1981, David played without astonishing success on the mini-tours in America, and so returned to play in South Africa. On his home circuit his game blossomed, earning him Rookie of the Year honours in 1981, and placed second in the Order of Merit a year later – an achievement which automatically qualified him to compete in Europe. Following a brief spell on the European tour between 1983-84 – the highlight of which was victory in the 1984 Cannes Open – David opted to play in America, and won his US Tour card in the autumn of 1984. With a reputation as one of the games hardest workers, David has since established himself as a multiple tour winner with the ability to produce exceptionally low scoring. In 1993 he played some of his finest golf to earn back-to-back victories in the Canadian Open and Hardees Golf Classic and win more than $1 million in a season. His career earnings currently stand in excess of $4 million.

Mentally, David is an exceptionally well organised golfer. He thinks clearly, sets himself realistic goals for each new season and prepares himself meticulously for each and every tournament he enters. He is a *feel* oriented player, and as such is inclined to experiment with his swing a little too much. But he concentrates on keeping the shape of his swing consistent right through the bag – and that's the key. Not overly long, David is one of the straightest drivers in the world, and a very crisp striker of the ball with the irons.

His is an uncomplicated approach: with a deliberate and rehearsed routine, he sets up to the ball, takes careful aim, and *turns*. So simple it looks like nothing can possibly go wrong. A fantastic bunker player and possessing great touch with the putter, David has the complete game, and when he puts it all together he is a fine golfer to watch. The following sequence illustrates beautifully the simplicity of his action, and for the average player this is a good model to copy.

Though he has yet to break into the major ranks, David Frost has the controlled swing and the temperament to attain golf's ultimate prize.

The swing:
compact and simple

When I wrote my first book – *The Golf Swing* – David Frost was the ideal model for the purposes of illustration. He follows the basic fundamentals, has a simple set-up position, makes a good turn back and a good turn through the ball, and swings the club on a consistent plane. On top of that he has good rhythm. David's build – 5ft 11in with fairly short arms and legs – is ideally suited to swinging the club in a simple compact manner, and this should appeal to many golfers.

David sets up in a very angular fashion at address – we can see a slight flexing in the knees, the rear protruding just a little, a straight lower back and just a slight tilt across the shoulders (**1**). He has a sound grip and plays the ball forward in his stance (which assists him in taking a shallow divot, as most good iron players aim to do), and his body alignment is excellent. The feet, knees, hips, shoulders and eyes all run parallel to one another. A tendency to stand fractionally too far away from the ball costs him full marks. But otherwise a textbook position, and one you should try to achieve. This is the one area of the swing over which you have total control, and the quality of your set-up position will determine how consistent your swing is. So work on it.

A natural right-to-left player, we can detect just a hint of an early wrist set as David swings the club away from the ball (**2**). With a slight rotary action of the hips, his chest and arms move away *together*, and by the time his left arm is parallel to the ground, the club is virtually fully 'set' (**3**). To complete his backswing, all David now has to do is complete his turn, which he does beautifully: as the right arm folds

1

2

3

4

away, we can see that the plane of the left arm virtually matches that of the shoulders. His short arms enable him to achieve this arm/shoulder relationship, and his compact three-quarter length swing with a full turn makes for a very solid, repeating position (**4**).

All I would say to David here is *keep more flex in the right knee* – one of his old tendencies is to straighten his right leg in the backswing.

David's 'back facing the target' look is complemented by a very simple lower body motion. With a slight lateral movement of his left side, he then initiates his downswing with an unhurried move, and as the arms fall nicely into the hitting area the club drops on to a noticeably shallower plane (**5**).

David maintains an excellent flex in his knees, and really stays down well with the shot through impact (**6**) as he releases the club with a

great extension through the ball (**7**) to a picture-perfect finish (**8**). This compact three-quarter type of swing produces crisp iron shots, and as a result of his hands being passive through impact, David is able to control distance extremely well. A pretty useful combination.

Interestingly, we can clearly see in these pictures the effect the address position has on the swing. I mentioned earlier that David appears to be 'reaching' for the ball, and indeed if we study

his position at impact, we can see too much of a gap between his hands and his body. This explains the odd errant shot – simply, the further your hands are away from your body, the more they are inclined to work on their own, and *vice versa*. This just goes to show that even great swingers of the club like David Frost are not immune from tiny swing flaws which, more often than not, can be traced to a minor error at address.

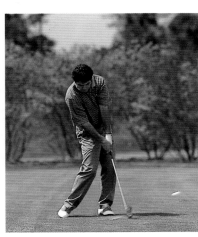

5   6   7   8

What you can learn from David Frost's swing

SIMPLIFY TECHNIQUE – KEY THOUGHTS TO TAKE TO THE COURSE

David Frost is very much a feel player – as opposed to being a mechanical player – and as with most people he can easily suffer 'paralysis through analysis'. So he tries to create simple feelings and images that enable him to execute his mechanics and take his practice-tee swing out on to the golf course. Simple thoughts free up the mind and allow you to play golf, as opposed to play *'swing'*. Too many technical thoughts only create tension and poor shots.

The following three examples help David – they might help you:

(*1*) **Focus on big-muscle movement:** To get the feeling of the body and the arms synchronising as they should, place a soccer ball between your hands at address and then move the arms and the ball away in conjunction with the movement of your chest.

Fling the ball over

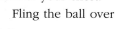

your right shoulder as you approach the top of the backswing, so that the ball flies to the left of the target you are aiming at. The feeling you should have is that the energy to propel the ball emanates from your chest – rather like an elephant swinging its trunk back. This is an ideal way to free yourself up, by learning to *swing* the club back, rather than 'take' the club back.

(*2*) **Sit into the right knee:** A key that David uses regularly, and one that I focus on with many players, is to 'sit' into the right knee at the top of the backswing. In other words, to *maintain the flex in the right knee as much as possible*. Winding the upper torso against the resisting right knee creates maximum torque, and the 'sit' thought acts as a buffer against swaying. It is a simple key that helps to produce a consistent top-of-the-backswing position and acts as a spring-board for a solid downswing.

(3) **Improve your line of approach:** Many good players tend to fight hooking or pushing the ball, which is often caused when the clubhead is approaching the ball on an overly in-to-out path, from too far behind the hands. A simple image to conjure up in your mind is one where the hands are working close to the body, but the clubhead is out in front of you – i.e. *outside* the line of the hands, as you see in this illustration (right). This pre-impact position will ensure that the club approaches the ball on a path that (once the ball is struck) will go left of the target line, thus enabling the player to hit the ball straight, or even create left-to-right-spin.

There are literally hundreds of images and feelings you could adopt. When you find one or two that work, keep a note of them. Your sensations can and will change, and reverting back to an old image or feeling can often help you to recapture your form.

HALE IRWIN

BORN: JUNE 3RD, 1945, JOPLIN, MISSOURI, USA. **TURNED PRO:** 1968. **HEIGHT:** 6ft (1.8m).

Hale Irwin won his first professional tournament at Harbour Town in 1971 – the Heritage Classic – on what is a notoriously tough, tree-lined, Pete Dye-designed course. His second victory occurred there two years later, and a year after that he captured his first major, the 1974 US Open at Winged Foot, a course recognised as one of the most demanding and remorseless tests in golf. Fast developing a reputation as a grinder, Hale exported his talent to win the World Matchplay Championship at Wentworth that same year, and returned to successfully defend his title in 1975.

Playing defensive back for the University of Colorado on a football scholarship clearly sharpened his competitive edge. Hale relishes tough courses because they make him concentrate and play hard. They suit his rational mind: with patience and tenacity, and the ability to hit the crucial shot at the crucial time, the consistency of his game accurately reflects his business-like demeanour. Between 1975 and 1978, he played 86 tournaments on the US tour without once missing a cut, and in 1979 that resilience won him a second US Open, at Inverness, Ohio. And while a select band of four men have won four US Open titles – Willie Anderson, Bobby Jones, Ben Hogan and Jack Nicklaus – only Hale Irwin has won three. Aged 45, he completed his hat-trick in some style, holing a 50-foot putt for birdie on the 72nd green at Medinah in 1990 to earn a play-off, which he won.

Hale's greatest strength is that he has no apparent weakness. Largely self-taught, he understands the principles of spin and ball-flight, and has the ability to adjust his swing according to what his senses tell him. Not a long hitter by modern standards, with a deliberate, controlled tempo he is able to produce a swing that repeats, and as he shapes and threads his way from tee to green, rarely gets into trouble. A natural left-to-right shape enables him to land the ball softly, even with the woods and long irons. Quite rightly, Hale is acknowledged as one of the finest fairway-wood players in the history of the game – a skill he put to good use in winning the Heritage Classic for a record third time in 1994.

It's in the hole! – Irwin celebrates his 50-foot birdie putt at the 72nd hole which earned him a play-off for the 1990 US Open at Medinah, Illinois.

With a single-minded efficiency, Hale has sustained his talents over a quarter of a century, and remains one of the game's most respected competitors. His unflappable determination makes him perfect matchplay material, and since his first appearance in 1977 he has played in five Ryder Cup matches, winning more often than losing. The highlight of that experience was his sensationally halved encounter with Bernhard Langer at Kiawah Island in 1991, which meant America reclaimed the trophy.

With a knack of playing tough courses well, Hale Irwin has more than twenty victories to his name, including three in perhaps the toughest of them all – the US Open.

The swing: *as the body turns, so the arms swing*

Even in still pictures, Hale Irwin's position over the ball oozes *'softness'*. This is a swing based around tempo and balance, and the motion stems from one of the most natural looking set-up positions I have ever seen. The stance is not overly wide, his feet appear to be angled nicely, and his arms hang relaxed from the shoulders (**1**). With a flexing of the knees, his body is poised and without tension.

Hale moves the club away with a very smooth one-piece takeaway (**2**), and the tempo established here determines the pattern of the entire swing. Against the flex in his right knee, he swings the club along a fairly flattish plane (**3**), then raises his arms to the top. He swings it *'in then up'*.

Turning his back on the target and the left shoulder under his chin, Hale places the club in a consistent slot at the top (**4**). The right arm is in a good supporting position, and he retains that softness in his left arm.

It is at this point that most players are susceptible to losing their rhythm, but not Hale. There is nothing rushed about his golf swing: as he changes direction, look at the way he maintains the flex in his knees (**5**). That subtle forward motion in the lower body

1   2   3   4

creates a 'lag' effect: as he unwinds, the right elbow works nicely in towards the right hip, and he achieves that sit-down, 'squat' position common to all good players (**6**). Using his legs like stabilisers, or shock-absorbers, that flexing in his knees helps him to stay down on the shot through impact (**7**), and he releases the club with a free-flowing arm swing as his weight moves across into his left side and he finishes with elegance and poise (**8**).

Study these pictures closely and you will notice that as he changes direction, Hale keeps the club swinging 'in front' of his body coming down. The arms, hands and club move on a path which is fractionally outside the path they originally travelled along on the backswing. This line of approach explains why Hale is a natural fader of the ball (the club never gets behind him, a problem most players dread, as it invariably leads to a hook).

With great balance in his lower body, Hale is able to produce a very consistent and repetitive swing pattern. The fact he stays down on the shot so well and keeps his head behind the ball at impact further explains his ability to sweep the ball off the turf with the long irons and fairway woods – one of the reasons why his game is so tailored to meet the demands of US Open courses.

5

6

7

8

What you can learn from Hale Irwin's swing

LESSON ONE: RELAX, BREATH EASY, AND SWING EASY

Lubricated with superb balance and tempo, Hale Irwin's swing features a wonderful blending of the arms and the body, and that quality stems directly from the position he achieves over the ball at address. It matters not what club he is using, when Irwin sets up to play, the manner in which he makes his grip and assumes his posture suggests a certain softness running through his entire body.

This is exactly what you must strive to achieve. Remember, tension creates all sorts of problems. Your muscles will only work for you if you allow them the freedom to do so. As you stand to the ball, you must encourage a similar *softness,* where the arms just *hang* from the shoulders, ready to swing freely.

Try this breathing exercise next time you go out to practise.

As you address the ball, breath in deeply through your nose and feel your chest expand. Then exhale out through your mouth just prior to you starting your backswing – if you can, try to exhale all the way through your swing to the finish (left).

The key is to synchronise the speed and tempo of your swing with that of your breathing. If you can do that you will find it difficult to swing in anything other than a smooth, repeatable fashion.

Many of my pupils find this an excellent way to forget about complicated mechanics and recapture lost tempo. Focus on one simple thought – such as fully turning your shoulders back and through – and concentrate on breathing out to start your swing. Once you achieve that softness at address, you will start your swing in a relaxed, smooth fashion, and all the moving parts will work together in sync.

LESSON TWO: FLEX THE KNEES, STAY *DOWN* FOR A SHALLOW SWEEP

One of the reasons amateur golfers find great difficulty in achieving a sense of consistency with the longer irons and woods is that as their anxiety increases, so does a tendency to want to *lift* the ball into the air. So often I see players who appear to straighten their legs on the downswing as they 'flip' at the ball with their hands. They never commit themselves to staying down with the shot, trusting their swing and allowing the loft of the club to get the ball up into the air.

With the long irons and woods, it's vital that you complete your backswing and simply let the clubhead *collect* the ball. This is Hale Irwin's trademark: keeping the flex in his knees, he stays behind the ball, maintains his height through impact and allows the clubhead to sweep the ball off the turf. His focus is on keeping a constant knee flex back down and through impact. To get the feel of this, hit some half-shots with a short iron, and sense the retention of the flex in the knees through

impact. Stay down with the shot, and in your mind's eye, sense that you see the clubhead striking the ball. Put your trust in the clubhead. After hitting a few shots, transfer these same feelings to hitting long irons and fairway woods. Pretty soon you should be sweeping balls off the turf in Irwin-like fashion.

TOM KITE

BORN: DECEMBER 9TH, 1949, AUSTIN, TEXAS, USA. **TURNED PRO:** 1972. **HEIGHT:** 5ft 8in (1.7m).

Although he has earned recognition as one of golf's all-time leading money-winners, the financial reward has long since ceased to be the motivating factor behind Tom Kite's astonishing record as a tournament professional. One of the game's hardest workers and inveterate tinkerers, Tom is driven purely by his determination to find out just how good Tom Kite can be. And his record suggests he's doing just fine.

Like so many players, Tom learned the game from his father. He grew up on a farm north of Dallas, and though his parents feared he might not have the physical makings of a touring pro, Tom never once doubted he would make it to the top. The benefits of the golf program at the University of Texas were soon evident. In 1970, Tom finished second to Lanny Wadkins in the US Amateur championship, and the following year won both his singles matches in the Walker Cup at St Andrews.

His patience rewarded, Tom Kite is finally No.1 at the 1992 US Open, Pebble Beach.

It was while at college in Texas that Tom met Ben Crenshaw. The two became great friends and adversaries, sharing national collegiate honours in 1972, and a legendary coach, in the late Harvey Penick. It was Harvey who instilled in Tom the discipline and self-belief that characterises his approach today. Taught that the object of the game was to *score*, Tom nurtured a determined competitive instinct and an appetite for practice. Upon turning professional in the latter part of 1972, he was voted Rookie of the Year in 1973, and in the years since has won more than 20 tournaments and accumulated more than $8m in official prize-money.

At 5ft 8in, Tom has had to work on conditioning and improving his swing to live with the ever-increasing length of championship golf and the distance modern pro's hit the ball. Not a powerful hitter, it is the sheer consistency of his game that makes him such a prolific winner and competitor. In every department he demonstrates an excellence born out of hard work and hours of practice. A player who has made the best of his talent, in 1992 Tom finally relieved himself of the sobriquet 'best player never to have won a major' when, aged 42, he controlled his game and his nerves in a buffeting wind to claim the 1992 US Open at Pebble Beach.

Tom's work ethic is an example to young players who dream of a career playing golf. His strength is that there are no real weaknesses in his game, and better than most Tom appreciates the deadly importance of the short game – the real *scoring* shots from 100 yards and in. It was Tom Kite who in the summer of 1980 attributed an up-turn in his performance to carrying a third wedge.

After studying the figures with short-game statistician, Dave Pelz, Tom decided that in order to achieve the versatility he needed around the green he would carry a sand wedge, a special 60° wedge and a regular pitching wedge. Thus was created the modern fashion of carrying a 'three-wedge system'. Tom practises this part of his game more than any other, and is rated as one of the finest wedge players in the business. The following sequence reveals his technique for immaculate control.

*An insatiable appetite for self-improvement and a sheer love of playing golf has made
Tom Kite one of the game's toughest competitors and prolific money-winners.*

The swing: *controlled body, passive hands*

The most noticeable feature of this wedge swing is that it is predominantly an arms and body action. There is little evidence of much wrist action, which is why Tom is able to so finely control the amount of divot he takes, a most important element in controlling distance. This is a swing governed by the rotation of the upper body. It is simple, efficient, and has no wasted motion.

It all starts from a 'no-frills' set-up position. We can see that Tom stands with his body slightly open in relation to the clubface-ball-target line, the ball positioned approximately in the middle of the stance, with his weight a little forward on his left side (**1**). From here, Tom moves the club, hands, arms and chest away *together* (**2**). Everything works in one-piece until about hip-height, when the weight of the club and the folding of the right arm set the club up (**3**). In completing what is essentially a three-quarter length backswing, Tom makes a good upper body turn over a relatively quiet hip and knee action (**4**). In perfect balance, he makes no conscious effort to transfer his weight to any significant degree – this is a shot of accuracy, not distance. In all, a very solid and clinical movement.

1   2   3   4

Reflecting perfectly his calm, placid demeanour, nothing is rushed as Tom changes direction. With a slight lateral movement of his hips and lower body, he makes a smooth movement towards the ball, and in natural succession his hands and arms drop the club into the hitting area (**5**). The consistent shape of

Tom's wedge swing is witnessed by the fact that the shaft plane both up and down perfectly match one another. As he swings through impact, his hands remain close to his body, the left hand leading the square clubface by quite a large margin (**6**). As the body continues to rotate through impact and the right knee 'bumps'

toward the target, the arms and hands swing through to a controlled full finish (**7**, **8**).

With great feel, Tom regulates the length of his backswing according to the length of the shot, and he is always conscious of accelerating positively through impact. Tom is in perfect balance throughout the swing, and has

total control of the clubhead.

Such is the simplicity of this action it appears almost as if Tom is tossing the ball into the air with his right arm – nothing more complicated than that. His shots land softly, with just a few feet of calculated roll – such is the finesse of one of the deadliest wedge players in the game today.

5   6   7   8

What you can learn from Tom Kite's pitching action

in turn produces consistent *feel*. These precision shots are primarily based on rhythm and distance control, the key being to position your lower body (i.e. your feet, knees and hips) slightly open in relation to the target line. This open lower body position enables you to make a relatively short swing and yet still get through the ball with a positive body action. Players who habitually set up with their body square to the target line usually end up 'flicking' at the ball with their hands – a method which can never be consistent. But with your body correctly aligned you can turn properly through the shot (the left side clears without restriction) and as a result you are on the way to developing a sound, repeating technique.

Tom Kite is the perfect model: to play a three-quarter wedge shot, he stands with his feet fractionally less than shoulder width apart, lower body open to the target line, and his weight slightly favouring the left side. Check your own set-up position with the help of a mirror. With your knees flexed and your body comfortably balanced, you should find that your arms hang naturally to place your hands a touch ahead of the ball, which for a regular pitch shot should be placed approximately in the middle of the feet. You are now ready to make a controlled pitch-swing.

LESSON ONE: PITCHING – PRE-SET IMPACT POSITION FOR GREATER FEEL AND CONTROL

The key to being a good pitcher of the ball is to set up to the shot in such a way that your address position promotes a nicely synchronised arm and body motion, which

LESSON TWO: LENGTH OF SWING THE KEY TO DISTANCE CONTROL

Great wedge players like Tom Kite have practised so much and developed such incredible feel for different length shots that they expect to hit each one close to the hole. That's the reward hard work brings. And while Tom personally likes to make a full follow through on all his wedge shots, I would suggest that the club golfer first acquaints himself with a scoring system based on the simple method of matching the length of the swing to the length of the shot.

Using a sand wedge for distances of up to 60 or 70 yards, think in terms of matching the length of your backswing with the length of your follow through. Keep things simple: make a smooth 'up and down' motion with the arms, linking them together with the movement of your chest, while at the same time keeping your legs calm for good balance. Remember, the key – as with the full swing – is to link your arm swing to your turn: if you make a quicker turn and a correspondingly longer arm swing, you will hit a fairly full shot; a slower turn with a shorter arm swing suggests a shorter, more delicate shot. Take these thoughts to the practice range.

The clock face analogy works well. Start off with a short swing, say from 9 o'clock to 3 o'clock, as you see illustrated on the opposite page (right). As you then increase the speed of your turn you will extend both the length of your backswing and follow-through (which you should consider a mirror-image). Imagine swinging from 10 o'clock to 2 o'clock, and from eleven through to one (left). Simply swing your arms back and mirror-image that position on the follow-through.

This image of the clock face really is a useful mental key, and as you practise and familiarise yourself with the distance each specific swing gives you, so your feel and control – and confidence on the course – will improve. It is important with all the different length shots to have a *smooth controlled acceleration*, which allows you to strike the ball crisply off the turf.

Practise different length pitch shots regularly – be aware of exact distances. Focus on good rhythm and vary the length of your swing according to the shot. I have no doubt that with a little hard work you will develop a magical wedge game and with it save yourself handfuls of shots.

BERNHARD LANGER

BORN: AUGUST 27TH, 1957, ANHAUSEN, GERMANY. **TURNED PRO:** 1972. **HEIGHT:** 5ft 9in (1.7m).

As the great writer and broadcaster Henry Longhurst used to say *'Once you've had 'em, you've got 'em'*. He reckoned without Bernhard Langer's self-belief and stoic determination – the German's strongest suit. Three times his game has been plagued by the fear which took away his putting – the 'yips'. And three times he has triumphed over that anxiety. With his trust in God, Bernhard's faith in life and dedication to his profession proved too great for something so trivial to stand in his way.

The son of a bricklayer, Bernhard was first attracted to the game as a caddie. Aged eight, with his brothers and sisters he would cycle the five miles along a wooded pathway from his home in Anhausen, to a local course, where he watched, listened and learned. In the summer school holidays, when the course was quiet, he played from dawn until dusk. A small, slightly built boy, Bernhard wielded the club with a ten-finger grip, and developed a long, flat swing. The club champion had a strong left hand grip. Bernhard copied him, and with a natural ability to hit the ball, turned pro four weeks before his 15th birthday.

Once again Bernhard Langer receives the famous green jacket – this time from Fred Couples – after winning the Masters in 1993.

His talent was soon rewarded. At 15 he played in and won his first professional tournament; two years later he won Germany's National 'Closed' Open; and in 1979, he cruised to victory in the Cacharel World Under-25's championship by 17 shots. All this time Bernhard played with a fear of putting – his 'nightmare' years – but with sheer mental and physical strength he persevered. In the summer of 1981, Seve Ballesteros recommended he try a heavier putter, and with renewed confidence, the ball started to disappear. In 1981, with a flurry of top-ten finishes and victory in the German Open, Langer topped the European Order of Merit. He headed the money list again in 1984, then packed his bags to develop his game in America.

Fittingly, it has been at Augusta National, home to the world's most treacherous putting surfaces, that Langer has vindicated his affliction. In 1985 he outplayed Seve Ballesteros down the stretch (and three-putted just once in four days) to win his first major championship, only the second European to win the US Masters. Most golf writers agreed this would be the victory to spur a glut of major titles, and yet while Bernhard has continued to win regularly around the world, and featured most prominently in a number of Open championships, it would be eight years before he claimed his second Major. Again proving his metal at Augusta, in 1993, his precise iron play and supreme putting touch – this time with a unique split-handed method – saw him lead from the front to be home by six shots for a second green jacket.

From tee to green, Bernhard is one of the most impressive ball-strikers in the game. His strong left hand grip might suggest a low raking hook but so hard does he practise that he finds a way to get the job done. Bernhard's philosophy is to think technique on the practice tee, but out on the course he clears his mind and thinks only about getting the ball into the hole. With exceptional feel he is a gifted bunker player and one of the finest chippers of the ball you will see. Whether he is playing well or playing badly, Bernhard never gives up trying, and with a strict command of his nerves he is, mentally, one of the strongest players in the world.

Germany's superstar player, Bernhard Langer is an inspiration to many of his countrymen, and indeed a role model for any aspiring golfer.

The swing: *strong grip, great compensation*

Like many tournament players, Bernhard Langer has a history of back trouble, and in recent years has made a few changes in his swing: first, to gradually ease the strain on the lower part of his spine, and second, like so many of the 'perfection'-seeking great players, to improve his technique.

Specifically, Bernhard's problems revolve around the fact that he tends to take the club inside and on a flat plane going back, for which he then compensates with too steep a plane coming back down. In his practice regimen he tries to reverse this trend – i.e. he works on *steepening* the plane of his backswing, so that he might correctly shallow it on the downswing, and thus make it easier on his back when he releases the club. In that respect, his swing – like that of every player – is continually evolving.

As we look at Bernhard's address position with a 5-iron, all appears fairly orthodox – except for the grip (**1**). Since he was a boy Bernhard has played with a very strong left hand grip (we can see at least three knuckles, and a distinct cupping in the left wrist), which he counters with a fairly weak right hand. In moving the club away from the ball, the effects of the grip can be seen in that the clubface is distinctly closed (**2**). Bernhard then works the club on a relatively flat plane around his body and there is a notable tucking of the right elbow (**3**). In conjunction with a full shoulder turn, he then lifts his arms in order to raise the club to the top of the backswing (**4**). The club appears slightly laid off (i.e. looking left of the target).

1

2

3

4

As he swings down his first movement is a lateral slide with his hips towards the target, in conjunction with an outward movement of his hands (**5**). This 'over the top' action steepens the plane acutely and forces his upper body to compensate by 'hanging back' and working underneath to get the club coming from the inside (this underneath move is what causes the stress on the back). This is where

Bernhard's naturally gifted ball-striking skills take over. As he stands up on the shot and loses his spine angle to make room for the club to release, he makes a supreme effort to hold his left hand square and firm through impact (**6**). While his body is technically out of position, his hands are passive as the arms swing through, and in this fashion he is able to hang on and plant the clubface squarely on the ball.

The fact that Bernhard's hands always *lead* the clubface explains why he is such a fine low-ball player, with a game particularly suited to the wind. As he moves through impact we can observe the way in which he tilts his shoulders and upper body on a steep plane in order to keep the clubhead travelling on line (**7**, **8**).

My opinion is that the more he works on getting his planes right, the fewer compensations he will

need to employ and the easier it will be for him to release his right side with a more level and less strenuous move through impact. With Bernhard's great work ethic, I would not be surprised to see his technique really improve as the years go by.

One thing is certain though: whatever faults may characterise this man's swing, they will always be overshadowed by the strength of his mind.

5 6 7 8

What you can learn from Bernhard Langer's swing

LEFT HAND MIRRORS
AND GUIDES THE CLUBFACE

While Bernhard Langer can be seen to be a little out of position with his plane and body through impact, the one thing he is really good at is returning the back of his left hand and the clubface squarely to the ball. This is why he is such an accurate striker of the ball, particularly with his short and mid-irons. After all, the most important position in any golf swing is that which is achieved at the moment of impact.

With instinctive awareness, Bernhard can shape the ball with the *feel* he has in his left hand. The subtle action of the left hand through impact can produce a draw, a fade or a straight shot to order – the mark of a world class player. Despite the compensations he is forced to make with his body, Bernhard knows that as long as he maintains control of the clubface with his left hand he can be aggressive through the ball, safe in the knowledge it will start on line. Bernhard regards the back of his left hand as the 'steering wheel' that mirrors and controls the position of the clubface. Ultimately, that sense of feel is what you must work to achieve.

This isometric exercise will help you to appreciate the sensation of the left hand returning 'flat' and square to the line of your swing at the point of impact, leading the clubface through the ball. Standing beside a wall, gently push the back of your left hand against it, as if you were rehearsing your impact position (left). Apply and gradually increase that pressure, and hold your hand in position for a few seconds. Feel and remember this sensation: it presents you with the feeling of what a square impact position should feel like, your hand *leading* the clubhead.

This drill is particularly useful to anyone who might be guilty of 'flipping' at the ball with a weak, scoopy hand action (right). It will help you simplify your thoughts, and with repetition will teach you to retain the lag between the clubshaft and the hands, and encourage a 'flat' left hand and square clubface through impact (far right). A simple feel drill, certainly, but one that can dramatically improve the quality of your shot making – picture it, feel it, and experience the difference.

Remember, for crisp ball-striking, the clubhead must not be allowed to pass your hands before the moment of impact – a must for low shots, playing in the wind, and ideal for pitching.

NANCY LOPEZ

BORN: JANUARY 6TH, 1957, TORRANCE, CALIFORNIA, USA. **TURNED PRO:** 1977. **HEIGHT:** 5ft 5in (1.6m).

Not even Jack Nicklaus can claim to have made such an opening statement as Nancy Lopez. In her first full season as a professional, the 20-year-old Californian won nine times on the LPGA tour – including a record setting five in a row – to be leading money-winner. The year was 1978, and with her dazzling play and brilliant smile, Nancy put women's golf on the front page. In a single glorious season, she stole the hearts of her adoring fans and raised the profile of the LPGA tour. The following year she underlined her arrival with a further eight wins – and even more money.

An outstanding amateur career had suggested nothing less. Born of Mexican-American parentage, her father, a keen single figure golfer, saw to it that Nancy preserved her naturally powerful and graceful swing. At 15, she won the USGA Girl's Championship, repeated that victory two years later, and earned her place in the US Curtis Cup team. While still an amateur, she tied third in the 1975 US Women's Open, and by the time she turned professional, in 1977, only the US Women's Amateur Championship had eluded her.

With an idiosyncratic rolling of the club away from the ball, and an *ultra*-slow backswing, Nancy is a very consistent striker of the ball, and plays with a repeating right-to-left shape. Once within 100 yards of the hole she is deadly accurate and has a great touch with the putter – a winning combination. On top of this her demeanour is such that she handles pressure superbly well. Rarely rattled on the course, she appears to maintain the same even temperament however she's playing.

While her record in regular tour events is second to none (with 47 LPGA tour victories) Nancy remains something of an enigma with only three major titles, each of which has been in the LPGA Championship – 1978, 1985 and 1989. But her impact on women's golf can never be understated, and in 1989 Nancy's achievements were recognised and rewarded when she was inducted into the PGA World Golf Hall of Fame.

In 1982, Nancy married baseball star Ray Knight, and with the arrival of their three daughters, golf is no longer the driving force in her life. And yet although her schedule has been increasingly restricted, when Nancy makes an appearance the crowds flock to see her, and beneath her smiling bubbly exterior remains a fierce competitive instinct. To cap a glorious career, Nancy would dearly love to win the Women's US Open – whether or not she achieves that goal, for as long as she plays she will remain a star attraction and a probable threat to win every tournament she enters.

Mention the name Nancy Lopez and you're talking about a legend, the player who did for the women's game what Arnold Palmer did for the men's.

The swing:
deliberate and repetitive

While Nancy makes a particularly idiosyncratic move to start her swing in motion, the one thing you can say with certainty about this action is that it is highly repetitive. This is born out by the fact that Nancy hits a consistent draw, and is always near the top of the table in the categories of fairways and greens hit in regulation. The ultra-slow tempo at which she makes her backswing, the momentary pause at the top and an excellent move through the ball all add up to consistency in her shot-making. And the smooth and deliberate rhythm reflects Nancy's calm demeanour and temperament – which is what a golf swing should do.

Nothing untoward about Nancy's set-up position (**1**). Her right hand grip is a trifle strong, but all in all she appears to be standing comfortably to the ball.

Nancy starts her backswing by rolling the club away with the hands in a very distinct fashion (**2**). There is little body motion early on, as depicted by the fact that her hips are still looking at the ball. This 'pushaway' movement with the hands, combined with the inward movement of the club, results in a flat backswing plane as the club works noticeably around her body.

The positive aspect of this unorthodox movement is that Nancy achieves a great extension and radius with her left arm. From a fairly flat position at hip height (**3**), the wrists then hinge the club up as she makes a full turn into her right side, while the ultra-slow

1

2

3

4

tempo of the overall motion enables her arms, body and the club to arrive almost in sync into a good position at the top (**4**). The path of her swing is such that the club points across the line – i.e. points to the right of the target. Also, as a result of Nancy's strong right hand grip, the clubface points up towards the sky in a closed position. This backswing position is typical of many leading lady golfers; being slightly across the line at the top encourages a free-wheeling downswing motion with the club approaching the ball on an inside path.

As she changes direction, Nancy's pause with the club at the top of the swing gives her lower body a chance to unwind first (**5**), and we can see that she makes a determined effort to get the weight moving off her right foot into her left side. Notice how early she is up on the toes of her right foot. Her aggressively clearing hips give her arms, hands and club plenty of space to release through impact (**6**). The club is moving on an inside path to the ball, is square through impact, and then once again is swung on the inside (**7**) as she continues to her finish. Nancy does a great job of staying *down and through* the shot, and this can be seen in her finish position, where you can see the slight bend or curve down the right side of her body (**8**).

Nancy's golf swing is a perfect example of building speed gradually and releasing it under control – very much a case of 'slow back', 'load up' and 'wait for it'. She lets the clubhead *gather* speed, and then accelerates through the ball.

5

6

7

8

What you can learn from Nancy Lopez' swing

**LESSON ONE: ACROSS THE LINE POSITION YIELDS
GREATER POWER, MORE DISTANCE**

Most lady golfers I teach would benefit from
getting the club across the line at the top of
the backswing. For a number of desirable
reasons: (*1*) swinging the club across the line
guarantees that the right side of the body
turns out of the way on the backswing; (*2*) it
encourages the arms to swing up; (*3*) it
enhances the swinging clubhead motion from
the top of the swing down and through
impact, and (*4*) it positively assists in the club
swinging on an inside path back to the ball,
which promotes a right-to-left draw shape,
and maximum distance.

To accomplish such a backswing position,
place a club on the ground next to your right
foot, pointing to the right of the target, as
you see illustrated. Then, as you reach the
top of your backswing, simply try to get the
club you are swinging aiming in the same
direction as the one laid on the ground.

When you achieve that you can be certain
you have completed your backswing, and
your game will benefit on all the points
itemised above. Get a friend to stand behind
you and give you some feedback – this is a
useful drill for ladies, seniors and anyone
who wants more distance.

LESSON TWO: TRANSFER YOUR WEIGHT, BACK *AND* THROUGH

I see many players who seem to hit the ball off their back foot, for the simple reason they are trying to *lift* the ball into the air. Automatically they hang back on their right side, with little or no weight transfer towards the target in the downswing. This leads to a very 'scoopy', powerless release of the club.

If you want to increase clubhead speed (and so up your distance) it really is critical that you transfer your weight correctly not only away from the target in the backswing, but to your left side as you swing through the ball. Do as Nancy Lopez does: push off your right foot and *'kick'* your right knee in as the club starts down, keeping your right elbow close to your right hip. This will increase both your hand and clubhead speed coming into the ball, and gets your weight moving over to your left side at impact.

A simple drill will help you capture the correct feeling. Place a golf ball under your right heel, and then as you make your swing, sense that your right foot comes up off the ball as you start down. Get used to this feeling with a few practice swings, then work into hitting some shots with a mid iron. So, to re-cap: turn back into your right side as you make your backswing, then push off your right foot as you start down. Let your weight flow back across to your left side. Allow yourself to balance up on the toes of your right foot at the finish – just like Nancy.

DAVIS LOVE III

BORN: APRIL 13TH, 1964, CHARLOTTE, NORTH CAROLINA, USA. **TURNED PRO:** 1985. **HEIGHT:** 6ft 3in (1.9m).

It was at a very young age that Davis Love III decided he would make a career playing competitive golf. His father, Davis Love Jnr – a fine player and renowned teacher who died tragically in an aeroplane crash in 1988 – had presented Davis with his first set of cut-down clubs when he was just 18 months old, and took delight in coaching his son from the moment he could walk. Golf was a way of life in the Love household, and Davis grew up in the rarefied atmosphere of the professional circuit. He never dreamed of doing anything else.

Davis Love and Fred Couples relax on Dorado Beach in Puerto Rico after jointly winning the 1994 Heineken World Cup of Golf.

A tall man blessed with a great deal of flexibility, Davis developed a classical upright golf swing as a youngster. His role model was Tom Weiskopf – a golfer with a classic swing in his own right. Thanks to his father his basic fundamentals were very solid, and he was able to hit the ball vast distances. Love attended the University of North Carolina where he earned All-American honours three times, and in 1984 won the North and South Amateur Championship. A year later he turned professional.

In his early years on tour, Davis' long and upright swing didn't bring him the consistency he needed. But as he has matured as a golfer, so he has worked on shortening and flattening his swing for greater accuracy and control. These changes might have cost him a little distance,

though you would never know it. With a deceptively easy swing, Davis is still one of the longest hitters in the game, and his accuracy with the iron clubs has improved immeasurably. He doesn't seem to exert any more effort than anyone else, but his long arms and legs act as such powerful levers that the ball seems to disappear into orbit.

As you study the sequences overleaf, the key ingredient for any student of the golf swing is the way in which Davis builds and maintains the width and radius of his swing arc. That is what enables him to use centrifugal force to develop such great clubhead speed and hit the ball so far with a very safe left-to-right fade.

Davis scored his first tour victory – the Heritage Classic – at the notoriously difficult Harbour Town course in 1987 (a tournament he would again win in 1991 and 1992), and an impressive resumé includes the prestigious 1992 Player's Championship. In company with Fred Couples, Davis has enjoyed great success representing America in the World Cup of Golf, monopolising the event between 1992 and 1994. At the time of writing, Love has yet to win a major championship, but there is no doubt in my mind that as his game matures further and he tightens up in certain key areas – notably with the putter and his wedge play – he has the potential to emerge as one of America's true superstars as we approach the next century.

One of the longest hitters in the game today, Davis Love looks certain to become one of America's true superstars into the next century.

The swing:

long levers, great power

A good role model for all tall players, Davis exhibits a fine posture and balance at address. He stands with his legs nicely flexed, left heel turned out a little more than the right, and with his chin perked 'up' (**1**). I like his comfortably straight lower back, and the fact that his weight is positioned on the balls of his feet – not forward on the toes. With his feet spread to shoulder-width apart, Davis sets up to the ball with his upper body slightly open in relation to the target, and that alignment helps him to produce a safe fade.

In conjunction with a slight turning of his head, Davis initiates his backswing with a wide one-piece moveaway and sweeps the club away along a natural path (**2**). There is no tendency to whip the clubhead dramatically inside the line or lift it prematurely up off the ground. Davis prefers to set the club naturally as the swing progresses (**3**), and the extension he achieves in his left arm explains his tremendous arc. Combined, these ingredients add up to produce an athletic and highly torqued position at the top of the backswing (**4**). Such is his flexibility that Davis is able to turn his shoulders twice as far as the hips – the left shoulder well under his chin, the club beyond parallel, and the left knee behind the ball.

From the rear, notice that 'floating' the right elbow enables Davis to achieve a very deep backswing position. With a relatively flat shoulder plane and upright arm swing, he swings his left arm well across his chest, and as a result has a tendency to get the club too much across the line at the top – but a swing of this

1

2

3

4

quality is allowed the odd flaw.

As Davis starts to move his left knee and hip to signal his downswing movement (**5**), the thing he really does very well is to retain the width of his arc approaching the ball – the key ingredient for distance and accuracy. In that subtle change of direction he shallows the plane of his downswing, and simultaneously maintains a fantastic wrist cock as the right elbow brushes his side (**6**).

With the club now in the delivery position, as the hips 'snap' open to face the target, Davis' left leg is forced to straighten under the sheer speed and pressure of the release.

His head beautifully still behind the ball, and left arm straight, Davis achieves a very powerful impact position (**7**). Many people believe a good impact position mirrors the address position, but as these pictures reveal, in a dynamic swing that's not the case.

Look at Davis: his hips and shoulders are very open in relation to the target – certainly not square. This rotary action of the body through impact maximises Davis' speed through the hitting area.

Having stayed down on the shot, Davis unwinds with a full and committed extension past the ball, the right shoulder rotating under the chin on the way to a very relaxed finish position for

someone who hits the ball so far.

On a specific point, notice how the position of the left elbow at the finish (**8**) is almost a carbon-copy of the position of the right elbow at the top of the backswing. This indicates how well the hands and arms are tied in to the rotary action of the body during the swing. And it is that synchronisation – along with his smooth rhythm – that produces powerful, on-line shots.

5

6

7

8

What you can learn from Davis Love's swing

LESSON ONE: WIDE AND CONSTANT ARC THE KEY TO LENGTH

Creating and maintaining a wide arc as you first approach the top of the backswing and then start down – combined with good balance and torque – are the key elements you need to encourage good extension of the clubhead through impact, and thus hit the ball a long way. No one does this better than Davis Love.

This isometric drill is designed to give you the feeling of having good arc width in your swing as you change direction from the top. As you see illustrated, stand a short distance from a tree (or a wall), and choke down on the grip of a mid iron. Make your backswing, then feel your hands and right arm push the butt-end of the club against the tree – maintain that pressure for a few seconds.

Do this several times, then move away from the tree and rehearse your swing in the normal manner. As you change direction, try to sense that you retain that same swing radius – imagine there is a good sized box-angle formed between the shaft and the upper part of your right arm as you swing down.

These feelings are exactly the ones you must try to recreate hitting shots – just make sure you keep your arms free of tension. Once you learn to retain that arc you will achieve maximum extension through impact and strike the ball solidly.

LESSON TWO: LEFT SHOULDER TO CHIN, RIGHT SHOULDER TO CHIN

A prominent feature of Davis Love's powerful swing is how fully he turns his shoulders, both back and through the ball. By contrast I see too many golfers who fail to complete their swing in either direction, primarily because they tilt their shoulders (as opposed to *turning* them), and don't trust themselves enough to turn their back fully to the target. Consequently they fail to release the upper body all the way through to the finish. This costs them both power and accuracy.

A swing thought that will encourage you to produce good body motion back and through is simply to turn your left shoulder under the chin on the backswing, and your right shoulder under the chin on the follow through. Basic advice which, if heeded, will ensure a full coiling and uncoiling of your upper body, a better weight transfer and a more powerful and on-line release of clubhead speed. Just saying to yourself slowly over the ball: *'Left shoulder, right shoulder'* will also encourage good rhythm and tempo during the swing.

PHIL MICKELSON

BORN: JUNE 16TH, 1970, SAN DIEGO, CALIFORNIA, USA. **TURNED PRO:** 1992. **HEIGHT:** 6ft 2 in (1.9m).

So much media attention surrounded Phil Mickelson's potential as an emerging star and champion of American golf that once he turned professional in 1992, the pressure was firmly upon his young shoulders. The boy with the Hollywood smile proved up to the hype: having earned his tour card and a two-year exemption without having to go to qualifying school – thanks to his victory in the 1991 Tucson Open as an amateur – he won four times in his first 18 months as a professional.

Interestingly enough, Phil is right-handed in everything but golf. When he first picked up a club, at the age of two, instinctively he copied his father, a right-handed player. And so evolved a classical free-flowing, left-handed action, as he mirror-imaged the shape of his father's swing in the backyard of their San Diego home. From that day his game has been built on pure natural talent, great imagination and a wonderful short game.

An outstanding junior career saw Phil win the US Junior Championship in 1988, at the age of 16. In 1990, while on a scholarship at Arizona State University, he then won the NCAA (National Collegiate Athletic Association) championship, and in the summer of that year won the US Amateur – so becoming

Hats off to Phil Mickelson for winning the 1995 Northern Telecom Open.

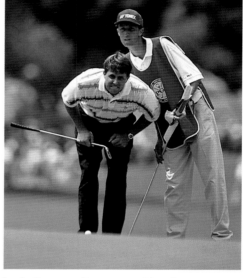

the first player since Jack Nicklaus back in 1961 to achieve that double, and the first left-hander to win the national title. His progress was no less spectacular on tour, with confident victories in the Buick Invitational and the International in 1993, the Mercedes Championship in 1994 – after a play-off with Fred Couples – and once again at the Tucson Open in 1995.

The quality of Phil's game is not only that he hits the ball great distances with a long flowing swing. His real genius is in his ability around the greens. Phil has great creative ability and absolutely no fear to hit tough short shots. For example, taking a long slow swing with a sand wedge to hit a soft floating shot to a tightly cut pin behind a bunker, and stopping it on a dime is for him a breeze.

A brilliant putter, he studied pictures of the great Ben Crenshaw to hone a silky-smooth stroke – he truly mirrors Crenshaw on the green, and rolls the ball beautifully. One of an elite band of *'twentysomethings'*, the anticipated rivalry between Phil Mickelson, Jose Maria Olazabal and Ernie Els should prove fascinating as we move towards a new era in golf.

Smiling all the way to the bank, it is simply a measure of his talent that boy-wonder Phil Mickelson was winning pro tournaments as an amateur.

The swing: *'syrupy' speed*

Phil Mickelson's swing is built around rhythm and tempo, and although he may exhibit one or two small technical flaws, his 'syrupy' motion more than makes up for them, and rewards him with a great deal of consistency. The problems he experiences generally occur with the irons, as someone with such a long swing might periodically expect. An excellent driver of the ball, Phil is one of the longest hitters on tour and plays with a natural draw shape.

Like all players who employ a long, flowing-style swing, Phil appears totally relaxed at address. He positions the ball well forward in his stance, shows minimal knee-flex, and has the distinctly tilted look of many left-handed players with the right shoulder appearing very high and with his head well behind the ball (**1**). As far as the grip is concerned he displays a very weak right hand and a fairly strong left.

If we look down-the-line, we see quite clearly that while Phil sets up with his knees and hips approximately square to the target line, his shoulders are slightly closed in comparison (i.e. aimed to the left of the target), and this encourages him to sweep the clubhead back quite sharply on the inside as he makes his initial move away from the ball (**2**). The unit of the club, the hands and the arms move together as one, while the hips and the left shoulder turn out of the way very early on. Following this inside move, Phil then proceeds to swing the club *around* his body, and sets the clubshaft on a very flat plane (**3**). Look at the way his right arm is extended here, the middle part of his torso winding up beautifully. From here, he completes his backswing with a very full turn, softening and bending his right arm and flexing

1

2

3

4

his left elbow to position the club at the top (**4**). The early inward move, that softening of the right arm and a tendency for the left arm to straighten, produces a long backswing, and one in which the club can be seen to point across the line. Phil is now fully wound up but he is also relaxed and looks to be in total control.

The change of direction provides a lesson in dispensing power: as he starts down, the right heel returns flush to the ground and

so begins the process of unwinding into the right side (**5**). His lower body *stabilises* the downswing – the legs appear so 'quiet' – and he retains the angle in his wrists as the arms drop the club into the impact area. The club swings down on a plane that is significantly more upright than that of the backswing and, holding steady with the legs, allows his arms to catch up with his torso.

Naturally right handed in everything but golf, Phil is then

able to hit purposefully with his left arm and hand, without fear of his right-hand side weakening and breaking down. Releasing the clubhead at terrific speed, he extends his arms and the club well past his body, the left heel staying on the ground through impact (**6**). The impression he sometimes gives of being a rather 'legsy' player is deceiving because the sag and bend in the knees occurs long after the ball has gone (**7**).

The arms and hands whistle through to a follow-through position which matches the backswing in terms of its poise and balance (**8**).

Phil has made one or two slight changes to his technique since joining the tour, such as firming up the hip action on the backswing and trying to generally shorten his swing just a little, and I feel certain he will continue to fine-tune his action.

5

6

7

8

What you can learn from Phil Mickelson's swing

LOOSEN UP FOR A
FULLER BACKSWING

In my day-to-day teaching I see a large percentage of amateur golfers who fail to complete their backswings, and who as a result have to *'lunge', 'chop', 'heave'* – you get the general picture – in order to hit the ball. These golfers will benefit from one of the most important lessons in golf, one which Phil Mickelson illustrates perfectly. It is simply this: if you can wind up, complete the backswing and stay free of tension, you can hit the ball a mile with relatively little effort.

My teaching philosophy places great importance on completing the backswing, coiling and building up torque with the big muscles in the body, so that the clubhead may be unleashed into the ball. A lot of players and particularly seniors – who may have lost some flexibility over the years – would generate a great deal more clubhead speed if only they knew how to make a few adjustments to make a complete backswing.

If you are lacking or losing distance, or feel you have no turn and a short backswing, try this.

I want you to focus on two aspects of your swing – first the movement of your left heel (speaking for the right-handed player), and the softness in a relaxed left arm while making a backswing.

As long as the right knee remains fairly anchored it is perfectly acceptable – and indeed necessary as you get older – to raise your left heel a little up off the ground in order to facilitate a full backswing (**1**). However, this raising of the heel must not be a

superfluous motion; in other words, just raising it off the ground for the sake of doing so has no benefit. It has to synchronise with a good hip and shoulder turn, just as it does for Phil Mickelson. The turning of the right side – and the inward movement of the left knee – should pull the heel slightly up off the turf. Now, if you combine it with a soft left arm, one that almost feels a little bent at the top, your backswing should have a look of fullness about it.

Having rehearsed your new backswing, the initial movement from the top – or your downswing 'trigger' – is the subtle *re-planting* of the left heel as you change direction (**2**). Don't rush down. This is where some players sense a slight pause at the top, but what they are really experiencing is an unwinding movement from the ground up, as the lower body leads the way before the hands and arms follow.

Once you develop an awareness for this longer and fuller backswing, and subsequent adjustment and timing as you swing down, you will experience a sensation of having more time

to hit the ball. Your swing will become smoother and as a result of more leverage and a bigger arc, you should hit the ball further with less apparent effort.

To further improve your

flexibility, a useful exercise is to turn the clubhead upside down, place your left hand below the right, and make some left-handed swings, *á la* Phil Mickelson. You might not look as good as he

does, but the swinging motion – especially the free-flowing, left-handed follow through – can only help to stretch out the muscles and thus further extend that backswing of yours.

COLIN MONTGOMERIE

BORN: JUNE 23RD, 1963, GLASGOW, SCOTLAND. **TURNED PRO:** 1987. **HEIGHT:** 6ft 1in (1.9m)

Few players can match Colin Montgomerie's astonishingly rapid transition from talented amateur to one of the world's top-ranked professionals. Having been around golf all his life – his father is the secretary at the Royal Troon club in Scotland – Colin won the Scottish Strokeplay and Scottish Amateur championships in 1984. While on a golf scholarship to Houston Baptist University, where he took a degree in business management and law, he was twice selected to represent Great Britain & Ireland in the Walker Cup matches. Not convinced he had the talent to make a living as a professional, Colin considered using his degree by taking a job in player management. However, he decided against that avenue, and it was a wise choice.

Since he took the plunge to turn professional, Colin's efforts in Europe have seen his position in the Order of Merit tumble from 164th in 1987 to consecutive firsts in 1993 and 1994. Earning Rookie of the Year honours in 1988, his first victory came in 1989, when he blitzed the field to runaway with the Portuguese Open by 11 shots. The consistency of his game not only makes him a regular top-10 contender in any tournament, but also a valuable member of the European Ryder Cup team, in which he has proved well-matched with foursomes and fourball partner, Nick Faldo.

Like another prolific money winner, Tom Kite, Colin's strength is that there are no apparent weaknesses in his game – he is accurate off the tee, keeps the ball in play, has a wonderful touch around the green and putts exceptionally well. Though at times volatile on the course, and often troubled by small irrelevancies, as Colin has matured he has developed the mental discipline of a major contender. Riding high on a wave of confidence after leading the Order of Merit in Europe for the first time in 1991, he almost sneaked the 1992 US Open at Pebble Beach. Controlling his game in the wind, 'Monty' finished on a level par aggregate of 288, thwarted only by the bravery of Tom Kite, who played inspired golf to win a thoroughly deserved first major. In 1993 the big Scot came closer still, finishing in a tie with American Loren Roberts and South Africa's Ernie Els, the latter eventually winning the play-off.

One of many: Colin Montgomerie with the trophy after winning the Spanish Open in 1994 at the Club de Campo, Madrid.

Colin is a big man with a full flowing, individualised type of swing. He assumes great control of the golf club, and hits the ball on a low piercing trajectory – perfect for windy conditions. His is what I would describe as a 'straight-line' action; for most of the swing the club works on a path that is fairly close to being vertical, and with natural feel he controls a safe, left-to-right fade – even under pressure. Famous on tour for his dislike of practice (the player and his clubs go separate ways between tournaments), 'Monty' proves that with the mental capacity to win, you don't need a textbook swing. Put another way, it's not how, it's how many.

Following an impressive amateur career, Scotland's Colin Montgomerie has made astonishing progress as a professional to become one of the game's toughest competitors.

The swing:

reliable up-and-down action

With a driver, Colin stands open to the target, and it is interesting that he portrays a very weak right-hand grip – i.e. the right hand is very much 'on top' of the club (**1**). The other unusual aspect to note is how far back in his stance Colin plays the ball – it looks as if he should be hitting an iron. What you must understand is that in most cases – and especially for better players – the ball position reflects the shape of the swing and specifically the path and angle of approach. In other words, the ball is positioned here for a reason, as we shall see.

Colin starts his swing with the butt-end of the club moving first (very much in the style of Payne Stewart), and in tandem makes a significant lateral movement to the right with his hips (**2**). The clubhead is drawn back in a slightly closed position initially, and the right arm remains extended and 'on top' of the left arm for a fairly lengthy period. As the swing continues, the club can then be seen to work up on a most vertical plane (**3**), and while the hips do turn, they also continue to move laterally away from the target – in fact, you could almost describe this as a sway.

Demonstrating great flexibility in his torso, Colin keeps his upper body 'centred' over the ball and his head very still as he completes his backswing with a full shoulder turn and a noticeably late – but full – cocking of the wrists (**4**).

From the rear view, the left wrist appears to be slightly cupped, and the vertical movement of the left arm has raised the left shoulder to such an extent that he covers his chin. With a swing that takes the club beyond parallel, the clubshaft

1

2

3

4

points to the left of the target, (i.e. in a laid-off position), while the clubface is fairly open (i.e. the toe hangs down).

As he changes direction we can see why it is so effective for Colin to play the ball back in his stance. With an instinctive reaction to his backswing position, he slides his hips forward as he starts the downswing (**5**), and adds angle to his knee flex while his upper body remains well back. The

arms, hands, and grip of the club approach the ball on a path well outside that of the backswing – hence the fade.

Holding the angle well between the shaft and his right wrist, Colin can be seen to work his upper torso back and 'under' the ball as he enters the hitting area (just look at how low his right shoulder is and how square his chest is to the target line). And yet, while his body is backing up, his left arm

and the shaft form a beautifully straight line at impact (**6**), and the clubhead extends low and long through the ball (**7**).

There is no question Colin is releasing the club with great speed, as he shows with his full extension and ultra-vertical follow through with the club resting on the back of his neck (**8**).

Colin's swing is very much a case of keeping his upper body very steady, and working his hips

back and through *underneath* that steady upper torso. [The ball position suits the relative positioning of his upper and lower body: if the ball were further forward, his lower body would have to slide even more for him to get to the ball.] And although his swing appears fairly 'wristy' at the top, through impact he has very *quiet* hands, which keep the clubface square – the reason he has so much control over the ball.

5

6

7

8

What you can learn from Colin Montgomerie's swing

LESSON: 'WRAP AROUND' FINISH PROMOTES A SOLID STRIKE

Although Colin is very much a left-to-right player, what impresses me is the way in which he

releases the clubhead aggressively to a full, high and balanced finish. Yes, he does swing slightly from the outside with the face fractionally open, but he is not *holding off* the release of the club through impact. He commits himself entirely to the shot and accelerates forcefully through the ball to hit what I call a 'released fade'. If he did not commit himself to such a complete finish, he would be prone to both slicing and pulling the ball.

Sam Snead always said he hit his best shots when he felt the club bounced off his back on the follow through. Many amateurs would benefit from this philosophy, as too many golfers are intent on hitting 'at' the ball, instead of swinging *through* it with a positive acceleration of the clubhead. High handicappers and slicers alike – players who tend to finish in a rounded and noticeably flat position – would certainly benefit from swinging the club all the way through impact to a position where the elbows finish nice and high and the club hangs down the back (right). Work on this image on the practice tee and you will encourage a more

powerful 'on-line' acceleration through impact – and so strike the ball more solidly.

DRILL: PUMP ONCE, TWICE, AND SWING TO A FINISH

Here is an excellent drill I recommend to help players hit *through* the ball – and not 'at' it. With a 6- or 7-iron, make your regular backswing, then slowly swing the club down to the halfway point in the downswing – i.e. to a position where your left arm is parallel to the ground, as you see in the illustration. From here, swing the club to the top again, then bring it back to this halfway position. Repeat this pumping action a couple of times, and then, on the third occasion, swing all the way through impact to a high finish.

The beauty of this drill is that it allows you to concentrate on *accelerating the club from the halfway point on your downswing all the way through the ball* and then on to a complete finish – exactly where the speed should be imparted.

JACK NICKLAUS

BORN: JANUARY 21ST, 1940, COLUMBUS, OHIO, USA. **TURNED PRO:** 1961. **HEIGHT:** 5ft 11in (1.8m).

Jack Nicklaus is the most successful golfer in the history of the game, and as such golf instruction was for many years based – rightly or wrongly – on his technique. Having won 20 major championships in a career spanning four decades it could be assumed that Nicklaus has discovered the 'secret' everyone else is searching for. Asked to share that wisdom, without hesitation Jack says it is the ability to keep a score going, even though he might not always have played particularly well. A modest statement, perhaps, but one which identifies perfectly the fact that, ball-striking aside, Jack Nicklaus has proved to be one of the greatest *managers* of a golf game that ever lived.

Easily the longest hitter of his generation, Jack's power off the tee enabled him to take full advantage of his precise iron play. Lost in a world of intense concentration, when he got on a roll he would make one birdie after another and literally overwhelm a golf course. But he had more than dominant strength. Mentally, Nicklaus was always one shot ahead of the game. With a strategy founded on realism, and adhered to with strict self-discipline, Jack played to his strengths. His length allowed him to reach most par-5's in two shots, but if he could not find the green he would lay up to leave a full shot at the pin. Similarly, he would calculate exact landing areas on all the par-4 holes: anything less than 100 yards was a 'part-shot', which he did not care for. So he deliberately eliminated them from the equation. His ability to hit iron shots the correct distance was almost uncanny, as his approach shots into the green would finish pin-high with monotonous regularity. Since the day he won his first professional tournament – the 1962 US

Open at Oakmont, after a play-off with Arnold Palmer – Jack's instinct has been to hunt major championships, and no man has ever proved to be more effective. Adapting his game to suit the changing conditions on either side of the Atlantic, his pure ball-striking enabled him to pierce the winds of the British Open, while at Augusta, his ability to hoist towering iron shots would prove to be the perfect antidote to hard and fast greens. And if the going was tight, as occurred at many a US Open, he simply left the driver in the bag, and let his 1-iron do the talking.

Jack Nicklaus holds aloft the Open trophy at St Andrews in 1978 – the scene of his third British Open victory.

If Jack had any weakness in his early years it was in his short game. His pitching, chipping and bunker skills never shared the brilliance of his long game – the reason being obvious: he did not miss many greens. But once on the green he always had a knack of holing the crucial putt at the crucial time, and those of us privileged to have witnessed the ageing of a legend will remember a career littered with the moments that have defined golf in the twentieth century. None was more dramatic than Jack's record sixth Master's victory in 1986, when at the age of forty-six he played the last 10 holes in seven under par to become the oldest recipient of the green jacket.

Business commitments and lingering back problems have tended to restrict his appearances in recent years, but Jack still believes he can win majors, even into his fifties. He wouldn't tee up otherwise. And on his rare appearances on the senior tour, he is most definitely the man to beat. Who would expect anything less from the player quite rightly awarded the title 'Golfer of the Century'.

Built on great power and strength, the technique Jack Nicklaus employed to win more major championships than any other golfer has been central to the way this game is taught and played.

The swing: *a deliberate building of power*

Jack pays attention to the basics in the golf swing, particularly the set-up. He would work hard early in the season on the fundamentals with his long-time teacher, Jack Grout. Broad across the chest, Jack is forced at address to 'hang' his upper body forward to some degree, but, over the support of extremely strong legs, he stands athletically poised, the left arm and the clubshaft forming a straight line (**1**). With naturally short fingers, all his career Jack has favoured the interlocking grip.

Jack is left eye dominant, and that characteristic turning of his head to the right as he finally prepares to move the club away from the ball has become something of a swing trigger over the years. And while the fashion among modern tour players is to 'set' the club early in the backswing, in Jack we see a much wider extension of the club away from the ball – a classic example of the deliberate one-piece takeaway (**2**). He turns the unit of his shoulders, chest, arms and the club *together*, and in so doing creates a tremendously wide arc on his backswing (**3**).

As he continues to turn his upper body away from the target, you can sense the coil building as he winds up the big back muscles. The shoulders and arms pull on the hips, which resist initially before fully rotating away from the target. A huge dynamic turn combined with high hands and supported by the often criticised 'flying right elbow' – no wonder he hit it so far. [Notice

1

2

3

4

how even though the elbow is high, it forms a 90-degree angle and the forearm is parallel to the spine.] The fullness of his turn positions the club across the line at the top (**4**).

Pay special attention also to Jack's footwork as he negotiates the transition. The left heel is pulled off the ground and the left knee is drawn in towards the ball as he completes his coil. Then,

with a distinct pulling motion with his left side towards the target, Jack stamps his left heel down to signal the change in direction (**5**).

With terrific strength in his knees and thighs, he resists fully unwinding his torso, as the arms drop naturally into the hitting position in readiness for the release. With that 'squat' look common to all solid ball-strikers, Jack retains the angle in his wrists

deep into the downswing, whereupon he unleashes his power into the ball (**6**).

Jack has wonderful extension through impact, as his arms swing past a *steady head* (**7**). This reflects on one of his key thoughts as a youngster, which was to keep his head still throughout the swing. The fullness of his turn in the backswing is only matched by the

fullness of his follow-through position: the hips rotate to face the target, while the club seems to recoil down his back, such is the speed unleashed (**8**).

Jack's fire-power – combined with his favoured and controlled left-to-right shape – gave him the ability to master any golf course. It is unlikely any player will ever dominate the game in such a way again.

| 5 | 6 | 7 | 8 |

What you can learn from Jack Nicklaus' swing

LESSON ONE: LOW AND SMOOTH START TO THE SWING

Although a wide one-piece extended takeaway does not suit everybody, one of the benefits is that immediately it emphasises the role of your whole body in terms of starting the backswing. Jack has worked on this principle all his life: in order to maintain a smooth tempo he makes a slow and very deliberate movement away from the ball. The fact that his wrists are passive late into the backswing multiplies the effect of this, and with a wide one-piece extension, the arms and body set off together.

This start to the swing is a fine lesson for all those golfers who cannot resist the urge to 'snatch' the clubhead away from the ball. Nothing is more likely to disrupt the rhythm and flow of a swing than an impatient hand action. In terms of your ability to build up a powerful backswing coil, the first few feet you move the club away from the ball are so critical: After you have made that initial one-piece start, it's not to say that you cannot cock your wrists – as many other fine

players do. The key – whether you set the club early or late – is to give yourself sufficient time to achieve the optimum blending of arm swing and body turn. A simple drill will help.

On the practice tee, adopt your normal set-up position with a mid-iron, but place a second ball about 12 inches behind – and slightly inside – the object ball. Then, as you make your

backswing, focus on smoothly sweeping the second ball away with the back of the clubhead, which naturally must travel low to the ground.

Controlling the motion with

LESSON TWO: WIND UP THE BACK MUSCLES, FEEL GREATER POWER

Another exercise I recommend to train a full left arm extension and backswing coil is the 'push-palm' swing, as you see here (right). Without a club, take your regular posture, but place the back of your right hand against the back of your left. Then, as you make your swing, sense that you push your left arm away with the right hand.

Feel your chest and back muscles winding up as your right arm folds and your left arm remains wide. Only when you achieve this powerful coiling of the upper body can you think in terms of unwinding *from the ground up*, as Nicklaus himself likes to describe the downswing sequence. Hold this position at the top for a few seconds in order to achieve proper

muscle memory. It is also a useful stretching exercise before playing or practising.

your shoulders and chest, simply turn the unit of your arms, hands and the club away *together* to create a wide arc. As that becomes natural to you, the small matter of turning your back away from the target completes a good backswing. In front of a mirror, check that your left shoulder is fully turned under your chin, and that the knuckles on your left hand reach up to the sky, as illustrated. This will ensure you are fully 'loaded up', with good width to your swing.

GREG NORMAN

BORN: FEBRUARY 10TH, 1955, MOUNT ISA, QUEENSLAND, AUSTRALIA. **TURNED PRO:** 1976. **HEIGHT:** 6ft 1in (1.9m)

The 1993 British Open championship at Royal St George's produced one of the great confrontations seen in recent majors. Laying to rest the ghosts that have haunted him in major championships, Greg Norman produced the most thrilling golf of his life to defend the challenges of Nick Faldo and Bernhard Langer with a last-round 64 to set an all-time Open record score of 269. The world's greatest golfers were at the peak of their ability, and Norman this time conquered.

Greg Norman simply exudes confidence. He is one of the most charismatic and exciting golfers ever to have played this game. As a star attraction he ranks alongside Arnold Palmer as one of life's showmen, a naturally aggressive man who can literally overwhelm a golf course. That marketable quality has brought lucrative contracts and endorsements, and it's a juggling act to split his time between his golf game, business interests and his family with homes in Florida and Australia.

A long-time friend and admirer of Jack Nicklaus, Greg attributes his early swing thoughts and playing philosophy to lessons he learned reading Jack's early instruction books. And there are many similarities in their technique. Like Nicklaus, Greg creates tremendous leverage in his swing with a wide one-piece takeaway, and while many of his peers work on an earlier wrist set, Greg creates tremendous power with a very late cocking of the wrists in the backswing. His strength and athletic physique give him 20 or 30 yards extra off the tee at any given time, and for that ability he has earned the deserved reputation as being one of the all-time longest and straightest drivers in the game.

Having won two British Open championships and more than 70 titles around the world, there is no question that Greg Norman is a class act. But having lost a handful of titles that really he had tucked away in his pocket, his resumé could and should be significantly more substantial. His career is littered with a trail of infamous happenings that might have weakened a lesser man: Bob Tway holed a bunker shot at the 72nd hole to deny Norman the US PGA at Inverness, Ohio, in 1986; from an impossible angle to the right of Augusta's 11th green, Larry Mize chipped in to do likewise in a play-off for the 1988 US Masters. In total, Norman has lost all four major championships in a play-off – the 1984 US Open, 1987 US Masters, 1989 British Open and 1993 US PGA.

Like many Australians, Greg was a great sportsman and surfer, and though from an early age he caddied for his mother (a noted low-handicap player), he would be 16 before he took to the game in earnest. Immediately a long hitter, he dropped his handicap from 27 to scratch in two years and turned pro at the age of 20. From the moment he first wrapped his hands round a driver Greg could smash the ball a long way, and tended to focus more on his full shots than developing his short game. In the past few years, however, he has worked extremely hard on honing his short game and putting skills, and has achieved a very high standard.

Greg's attacking style of play yields a flush of birdies and eagles, but critics argue that at times he is *too* aggressive, and that a more cautious approach might be better. In recent years he has not only worked on his swing but also on a fitness program he hopes will extend his playing career at the highest level. With a desire for perfection, Greg is still learning and improving. More dangerous than ever, 'The Shark' is in mature waters, and has the capability to go on winning major tournaments for years to come.

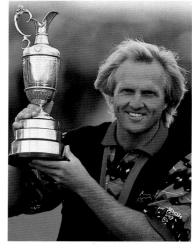

The calm after the storm – Norman was unstoppable in the 1993 British Open at Royal St Georges.

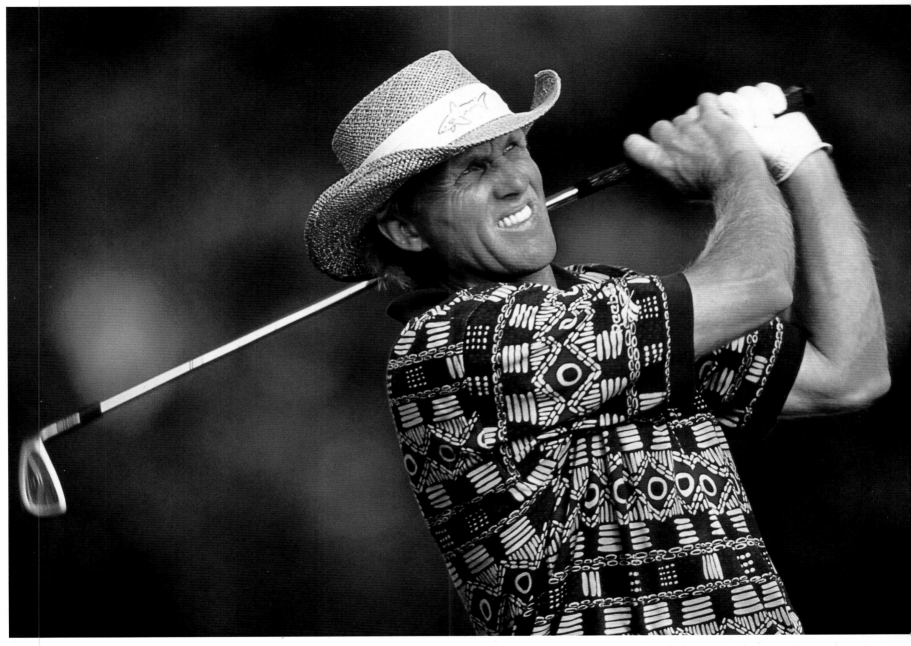

Though Lady Luck has not always been kind, on the course he feels nobody can beat him. And that self-confidence makes Greg Norman the champion he is.

The swing: *dynamically controlled power*

In the early years, Greg's swing was longer and more upright than you see it today. In an effort to gain more control – especially with the irons – he has worked hard on shortening and flattening his swing to make it more compact and reliable.

This is an excellent athletic set-up position to copy (**1**). The chin is up, the lower part of his back is in a straight line and the hands hang in a neutral position. One of the subtle changes Greg has made is in the width of his stance, spreading his feet to the full width of the shoulders. Combined with an ample knee-flex, this provides a solid platform; one that enables him to wind and unwind his body in balance. Notice also the way in which he hovers the clubhead behind the ball at address – another distinct Nicklaus influence.

With the club moving away from the ball in conjunction with his hands, arms and shoulders, Greg exhibits a classical, wide, one-piece takeaway (**2**). As the movement progresses the width and extension of Greg's backswing is clearly visible: the club on a much flatter plane at the halfway stage than it used to be, due to there being slightly more rotation in the left arm (**3**).

But the late setting of the wrists is very much a Norman trademark, and the resistance in his lower body is quite tremendous – you need to be physically strong to imitate this.

Against that resistance of the lower body, Greg continues to wind his shoulders and upper body through a full 90°. Notice that the knees hardly move at all – further proof that this is a tremendously torqued backswing position. The weight of the clubhead finally exerts its influence on his wrists, and although the club may be a

| 1 | 2 | 3 | 4 |

little shut and across the line at the top, the compactness of this swing is there for all to see (**4**). This dynamic position could only be described as *fully loaded*.

Greg's first move down is simple: his body remains essentially passive, and of course without wasted motion, there is no wasted energy. That's the key. The left side of his body initiates the unwinding process – the left knee followed by the left hip and left shoulder, moves towards the target, and the arms drop into the perfect position from which to deliver the clubhead to the ball (**5**). At the same time the left shoulder moves away from the head, and the arms drop into a perfect hitting position. Greg *stresses* the shaft tremendously coming down, and the leverage that he has built up through the delayed uncocking of the wrists – coupled with the wide arc that he maintains – really allows him to explode through the ball (**6**).

The powerful lateral move with his left side causes his upper body to hang back somewhat through impact and a slight curve can be seen in Greg's torso as his arms fully extend through the ball (**7**). This position certainly assists him in sweeping the ball off a tee with the driver – and explains why he takes such shallow divots with the iron clubs. And there is no holding back as the club is whipped through to a very full, but balanced, follow-through position (**8**).

Greg's strength and ability to keep the hands quiet through impact explain why he is able to deliver the clubface squarely and consistently to the back of the ball – and is why he is such a great driver of the ball. As a result of this contact, he hits the ball on a very straight flight, although he likes – and has the skill – to work his shots in either direction, depending on the situation.

5

6

7

8

What you can learn from Greg Norman's swing

LESSON ONE: A DRILL FOR A STRONG, ATHLETIC POSTURE

I want you to focus on the way Greg positions his body to the ball – he is extremely 'athletic'. With his feet turned out – the left slightly more than the right – the knees are flexed and slightly pinched 'in', supporting the weight of the trunk. The lower part of his back is comfortably straight, while the chin is positioned nicely up so that his shoulders have room to turn freely. In short, an excellent address position from which to synchronise the first move away from the ball.

Getting your posture correct is something you must strive for, because the angles formed are the foundation of a repetitive golf swing. This drill will help you. With your feet stance-width apart, place your hands on your hips and slowly get yourself into a squatting position, in the fashion of this illustration. Sense the pressure on your thighs, and then gradually raise yourself up, straightening your knees while maintaining a straight lower back.

Keeping your chin reasonably erect, raise yourself to a position in which your knees are slightly flexed and you feel some pressure in the lower part of your back and on your thighs. Finally, place your hands in front of you, as if to assume hold of a club.

Do this regularly and you will achieve the desired athletic set up position, as you see illustrated here with the driver (right). A full-length mirror will help you monitor your progress.

LESSON TWO: KEYS FOR GREATER DISTANCE

Two things that impress me about Greg's swing: *(1)* the way he moves everything away *together* from the ball, and *(2)* the resistance that he creates in order to build up his tremendous torque on the backswing.

(1) **Knees hold the key to resistance:** A simple thought for creating resistance on your backswing with your lower body is to imagine that the gap formed between your knees at address is retained as you reach the top of your backswing. This solid knee and lower body movement will allow you to wind up your upper torso like a spring. Combine this with everything moving away together, and you will soon be ripping your tee-shots like Greg!

(2) **Promote co-ordinated movement:** A great way of developing the feel for the club, arms and torso to move away as a unit is to place a large ball between your elbows, resting slightly on your chest. Make a number of practice moves, moving the ball and your chest away together. Do this a few times, keeping the ball in place as you turn your arms hand and chest to about waist high. If you want to hit shots with this drill, be aware that the ball should fall out as you swing past that halfway position.

1

2

JOSE MARIA OLAZABAL

BORN: FEBRUARY 5TH, 1966, FUENTERRABIA, SPAIN. **TURNED PRO:** 1985. **HEIGHT:** 5ft 10in (1.8m)

Among Jose Maria Olazabal's first memories as a child are the hours he spent on the putting green at the Real Club de San Sebastian, near his birthplace of Fuenterrabia in the Basque region of northern Spain. Born into a family of proud golfing tradition – both his father and grandfather were green-keepers – playing and watching the game was a natural part of daily life. And, as if to serve notice of what was to come, Jose took the Spanish under 9's championship at San Sebastian, aged seven.

Scratch by the time he was 15, Olazabal's *curriculum vitae* confirms excellence at every level. He won the British Boy's championship at 17, the British Amateur at 18 (beating Colin Montgomerie in the final), and the British Youth's at 19 – the only player ever to win the Amateur Triple Crown. With nothing left to prove, the Prince of Spanish golf turned pro at the end of 1984, and in 1985 finished top of the class at the qualifying school. The following year he won twice to finish second on the European Order of Merit, and was voted Rookie of the Year.

Before he reached his 25th birthday, Olazabal was a multiple winner around the world, and though on paper his transition from amateur sensation to the sharp end of professional golf would appear effortless, it is no coincidence that the Spaniard is one of the most dedicated and hard working players in the game. While his magical touch on and around the green seems to look after itself – Ballesteros himself rates Olazabal as the best putter in the world from inside 10 feet – his swing,

characterised by a weak grip and a fierce rhythm, requires a considerable degree of maintenance. Like a finely tuned engine, there is no wasted motion in his action, and when he finds the necessary blend of arm and body speed he flights the ball with mesmerising accuracy. That skill was crystal clear in 1990, as he produced a rush of some of the most sensational golf ever seen on the US Tour to win the World Series by 12 strokes after a blistering nine-under par opening round of 61, which he followed with three consecutive 67s.

With the heart of a lion and the courage of a man who has tasted *real* pressure, Olazabal has a competitive maturity far beyond his years. At just 21, he played the starring role to help Europe win the 1987 Ryder Cup at Muirfield Village – the first ever

Superlative iron play and a clinical putting touch won Jose Maria the 1994 Volvo PGA Championship at Wentworth, England.

European victory on American soil – and his record reads 13 wins in 20 matches. Forming a devastating partnership with Seve in that head-to-head arena has sharpened his mental edge to the point where he believes he can beat anybody. In 1994, at the age of 28, he *did* beat everybody, holing a decisive eagle-putt at Augusta's 15th hole on Master's Sunday to win a thoroughly deserved first major championship.

As he has acquired the necessary length to complement his famed short game, Jose Maria Olazabal has emerged from the shadow of his countryman, Seve Ballesteros, as a player of world standing.

The swing:
weak grip, fast action

Jose Maria Olazabal takes care of the fundamentals beautifully. He is thoroughly consistent in his routine of aiming the club, taking his stance and assuming a good posture – the elements that relate directly to the quality of impact. The most noticeable feature in what is otherwise a perfectly orthodox address position is Jose Maria's weak left hand grip (**1**). In recent years he has actually tried to strengthen the position of his left hand slightly (i.e. turned it clockwise on the club) to reveal more knuckles. However, it is still one of the weakest grips in modern golf.

In moving the club away, we can see the extension Jose Maria achieves as he turns the unit of the arms, shoulders and chest 'together' (**2**). There is no rotation of the left arm or the clubface – indeed the face is closed and remains looking at the ball during the early stages of the backswing.

With a very brisk tempo, he controls his swing with the rotary motion of the upper body, and as his left arm is drawn tightly across the chest the right arm folds snugly into his side (**3**). Against the resistance in his knees and hips, Jose Maria winds his upper body like a spring to arrive at the top with his shoulders turned way beyond 90°, his hips less than half that, and the clubface looking at the sky, again in a closed position. From the rear view, we can see just how the compact and *connected* look of Jose Maria's arm swing and shoulder turn (combined with the tucking down of the right elbow) leads to a fairly flat arm and shoulder plane (**4**).

A distinct chain reaction marks Olazabal's transition: the hips and knees slide laterally towards the target as he pulls his left shoulder away from his chin (**5**). At the same time his left arm works down his chest and slightly out towards the ball (compare this with the corresponding position

1

2

3

4

on the backswing). Notice also how well he retains the angle between his right wrist and the clubshaft deep into the down-swing. To offset the forward sliding motion of his lower body, he makes a conscious effort to keep his head behind the ball as he approaches impact – much like Seve Ballesteros.

Naturally aggressive, Jose Maria really does rip through impact (**6**). As his body continues to rotate and clear away, the left leg straightens to support the hit. We can see that one of the benefits of his weak grip (and this is reminiscent of that great iron player Johnny Miller) is that the back of the left hand is perfectly square to the target as the clubhead meets the ball – a key factor in explaining his pinpoint accuracy with the iron clubs. Free-wheeling to a finish, Jose Maria exhibits great extension with his right arm as his right side 'chases' the ball all the way through to the target (**7, 8**).

While he achieves a dynamic position at the top of his backswing, it is interesting to observe that within this motion Olazabal does suffer a tendency to tilt his hips towards the target in what I would describe as a slight reverse-pivot type of situation. Such a body action is fine for the iron clubs, as it produces the desired downward angle of approach necessary to pinch the ball crisply off the turf, and indeed Jose Maria is an excellent iron player, comfortable working the ball in either direction.

His problems generally arise with the straight-faced driver. At times, that slightly reversed position at the top, with a closed clubface – combined with a tendency to slide his legs forward and 'hang-back' with his upper body on the downswing – makes it tough to flight the ball consistently. His move produces more of a *descending* angle, as opposed to the sweeping action required by a driver. As his swing continues to evolve, this is something I am sure Jose Maria will work hard to rectify.

5

6

7

8

What you can learn from Jose Maria Olazabal's swing

PRE-SET DRILL TEACHES YOU THE BENEFIT OF 'LINKAGE'

One of the reasons Jose Maria Olazabal is so accurate with his iron play is that his swing is so beautifully compact: it appears as if he simply turns his shoulders away from the target, and then turns through to face it. What I really like is the way he links together the movement of his arms and the club with the rotary action of the body – i.e. the big muscles in his torso control the smaller muscles in the hands and arms. Or, as I like to term it, *'The dog wags the tail'.*

The problem many players have is that their arm swing and body turn tend to work *independently* of each other – i.e. the components of the swing are out of 'sync'. I see evidence of this all around me on the practice range. Failing to properly link together the swinging of the arms with the rotary motion of the body, there is no consistency in the release pattern through impact, and their ball-striking is erratic.

So how do you synchronise

all the moving parts?

This pre-set drill will teach you the sensation of swinging your arms and turning your torso in harmony (left), and putting you in a perfect slot at the top of the backswing. With a mid-iron, take your normal set up position, and then without moving your arms, hinge your wrists to the right until the clubshaft reaches a position parallel with the line across your toes. Without any further manipulation of the hands, all that remains is for you to then turn your left shoulder under your chin. Your cue: *pre-set* the club, check it, and then *turn* the shoulders.

Hit a few shots with this procedure. From this pre-set address position, you should really sense the bigger muscles in your upper body winding and coiling. This will create the linkage between your arms and your body so necessary for solid and consistent ball striking.

Another good image to have is that of swinging the club in a room with a very low ceiling (right). In tandem with the benefits of the pre-set drill, this mental exercise helps you to eliminate any tendency to 'lift' the arms in the backswing, and so promotes a full turn married to a short, compact arm swing. The result? Superior control of both the distance and trajectory of your shots.

NICK PRICE

BORN: JANUARY 28TH, 1957, DURBAN, SOUTH AFRICA. **TURNED PRO:** 1977. **HEIGHT:** 6ft (1.8m)

Nick Price played many sports as a boy, and he was good at all of them. That all-round versatility enabled him to develop the hand-eye co-ordination so important in sport, a gift which Nick eventually decided he would apply wholly to golf. He grew up in Zimbabwe, formerly Rhodesia, and fine-tuned his game as a youngster on the courses in Southern Africa.

Ever since the day he won the World Junior championship in San Diego in 1974, Nick was always destined for greatness. He often talked about turning pro, though his decision to do so was put on hold in 1976, while he served for two years in the air force – a period which instilled a deep-rooted mental and physical discipline: the very qualities of a major champion. Nick learned his trade on the European tour from 1978 to 1981, but not being a lover of cold weather, he then decided to move to America, where the conditions better suited his game. He earned his US tour card in 1982, and that same year might have won the Open at Royal Troon.

Nick was just 25 when he played himself into contention to win golf's oldest championship, and only his inexperience denied him. Though he dropped four shots over the closing six holes to let Tom Watson in through the back door, he at least proved to himself that he was capable of reaching that centre stage. In 1983, in his first year on the US tour, he qualified for the World Series of Golf as the leader of the South African Order of Merit, and went on to win by four strokes from Jack Nicklaus, thereby ensuring a 10-year exemption in America. Fuelled on in that knowledge he worked relentlessly on his game and in 1988 again found himself heading the leader-

Nick Price with the US PGA trophy, which he won for the second time in 1994.

This birdie putt at the 16th – followed by that famously outlandish eagle at Turnberry's 17th hole – earned Nick Price British Open glory in 1994.

board at the Open, this time at Royal Lytham. There, he protected a two-shot advantage with a superb closing round of 69, with which ordinarily he would expect to have been crowned the champion. But that year Seve Ballesteros produced one of the finest inspired rounds in history – a flawless 65 – to pip Nick at the post.

To the surprise of no one, Nick finally won his first major in 1992, the US PGA Championship, a victory that spurred a phenomenal blitz of golf. With a knack of making things happen, he won six times and was player of the year in 1993. In 1994 he then constructed a vintage season, with seven wins, including the most dramatic victory in the Open with *that* 55-foot eagle-putt on the 71st hole at Turnberry. A month later, the 37-year-old won the US PGA championship for a second time at Southern Hills – the first man since Tom Watson in 1982 to win consecutive major championships. Nick's game had reached such a level of excellence he was accorded superstar status; his ball-striking, short game, putting and – most importantly – his confidence came together to make him the number one player in the world.

A love of watersports has enabled Nick to maintain a high level of fitness, and with great upper body strength and a vice-like grip, he swings the club like it were a tooth-pick – his customary sharp waggles say it all. The swing is quick, and so by nature is Nick. But if the arms and body work in 'sync', it's difficult to swing the club *too* fast. A quick tempo, yes. But great rhythm. Nick has one of the most compact, repeating swings in golf, and the ball comes off the clubface like a bullet. There is no purer ball-striker in the game today.

One of the game's late bloomers, Nick Price is enjoying the fruits of a career founded on natural talent, and polished brilliantly with sheer hard work.

The swing: *aim and fire!*

Like all great players, Nick Price keeps a close eye on the details of his set-up position, and this is a fine model to copy (**1**). He stands well balanced, with his weight spread over the middle of his feet. While his strong forearms and big hands appear to be in total control of the club. I particularly like the angles he creates in his body – knees nicely flexed, hips square to the target and the right shoulder

set slightly lower than the left. The bow-legged look he has indicates the strength in his legs – the muscles in his thighs are braced – and that helps him pack the resistance in the lower body.

With a firm grip and aggressive tempo, he does not wait around at address. He gets on with it, and moves the club away from the ball smartly with a solid, one-piece motion (**2**). This extended one-piece movement helps Nick to pace his arm swing with his turn

on the backswing, and also helps to get his weight moving into his right side. An earlier wrist set would not suit his natural quick tempo, and would ruin his timing. Look at how the triangle, formed between his arms and shoulders, turns perfectly intact.

The area that Nick pays most attention to in his swing is from this moveaway to the initial start

of the downswing. His tendencies, or faults, are to get the clubface a little too closed, and the shaft plane a little too steep. To counter this his thoughts are to *rotate* the club and the left arm on plane, such that an extension of the butt-end of the club points between his feet and the ball (**3**), from where he tries to cock his wrists fully as he reaches the top.

1

2

3

4

To 'sit' and flex into his right knee, and to keep his left hip and left shoulder high are some of Nick's key thoughts, and he has really improved in these areas over the years. You can almost feel the resistance in the lower body as he winds his upper torso like a spring (**4**). From face on, although Nick does not have the greatest of flexibility, we can see that he moves well behind the ball with a very full shoulder turn.

Allowing his right elbow

the freedom to work away from the side of his body, the club is supported in a beautifully square position at the top.

One of the most talked about aspects of Nick's action is the way he shallows his swing plane as he changes direction. From a fairly upright backswing plane, his hands drop as his body begins to unwind (**5**), and as the right elbow starts to work down in front of his chest, gravity pulls on the clubhead, shallowing it out to a

point where the club is beautifully on plane as it approaches the ball (**6**). As long as Nick keeps his legs passive (indicated by the fact his right foot is just about flat on the ground through the impact area) he is now able to unwind his arms and the club in sync with the turning of his body. Nick likes to feel as if he is *'throwing'* the clubhead from the top of the swing with his right hand. The reason? This tends to neutralise his problem of pulling too hard from

the top with his left side, causing the club to shallow too much – a problem most players would pay a lot of money for.

With his head steady, Nick retains his spine angle through the shot (**7**) and is able to release his right side and chest aggressively towards the target, keeping his hands very passive and quiet (**8**) – which he does with machine-like regularity.

5

6

7

8

127

What you can learn from Nick Price's swing

SHALLOW YOUR DOWNSWING FOR A POWERFUL RELEASE

Technically speaking, the most noticeable feature of Nick's swing is the way he so deliberately sets the club on a fairly steep plane going back, only to shallow it out from the top to approach the ball on the desired inside path. By contrast, I see far too many amateur players who do the opposite: rolling the clubhead away from the ball on an overly flat plane (right), they are forced to *lift* the club to the top, the usual result being a steep downswing plane – i.e. the clubhead approaches the ball too much from the outside, which leads to all manner of bad shots.

In an ideal world, the club would travel up and down on the same plane: the perfect *repeating* golf swing. But such precision is not humanly realistic, basically because of the number of moving joints required to swing a golf club. The key to a consistent swing is getting the golf club approaching the ball on a plane which pretty much mirror-images the angle of the club as it was set at address. And it is far easier to achieve this downswing plane

when you set the club slightly steeper on the backswing. Then, assuming a correct body motion, gravity can play its part in pulling

the club down onto a shallower plane.

Try the following mental imagery.

the club. In Nick's swing, on the previous spread, you can see the shaft has shallowed to a point where it is virtually parallel to his right forearm at the halfway down position. This is ideal. Use a mirror to work on this shallowing process – check halfway back and halfway down.

Practise this often, and you should find that the improvement in your downswing plane will greatly enhance the quality of your ball striking.

Another drill I suggest you try to encourage this shallowing of the plane in the downswing is to stand next to a wall or door frame, place your right elbow against the wall – as you see illustrated below – and then exert forward pressure from the lower part of your elbow. This isometric exercise will train your right elbow to move down and in front of your chest – exactly as it should in the swing itself.

In front of a full-length mirror, take your set-up with a mid-iron, then focus on setting the club on a fairly upright backswing plane, so that halfway back the butt-end points between your feet and the spot where the ball would be. Complete the backswing, and then as you begin to unwind your lower body, shallow the plane of

PAYNE STEWART

BORN: JANUARY 30TH, 1957, SPRINGFIELD, MISSOURI, USA. **TURNED PRO:** 1979. **HEIGHT:** 6ft 1in (1.9m)

Resplendent in his trademark plus-fours (or 'knickers'), dressed from head to toe in the vivid colours of the National Football League of America, Payne Stewart possesses one of the most distinctive and classically-shaped golf swings of the modern era. With what Ben Crenshaw describes as the 'best turn in golf', the quality of Payne's swing is its supple grace. In full flight, you might easily be watching the flowing action of a past master – a Walter Hagen or Bobby Jones. Dancers work with the rhythm of their feet, and Payne appears to utilise a similar skill – as if his swing was set to music.

Like Jimmy Demaret and Doug Sanders before him, classic dressers of yesteryear, Payne Stewart has earned the right to stand out from the crowd. Upon graduating in business studies following a golf scholarship at the Southern Methodist University in Dallas, Payne turned professional in 1979 and developed his game for two years on the Far East Asian circuit. He competed there successfully, winning the Indian and Indonesian Opens, and finally securing his US tour card at the qualifying school in the autumn of 1981. Drawing on his overseas experience, Payne quickly forged a reputation as a contender, winning the Quad Cities Open and Walt Disney Classic in his first two seasons. And yet the art of winning did not come easily.

For much of the 1980s, Payne Stewart was a good player who seemed unable to finish tournaments. A solid ball-striker, he appeared to relish playing under pressure, and yet visits to the winner's enclosure were few and far between. He finished runner-up to Sandy Lyle in the British Open at Sandwich in 1985. In the 1986 US Open at Shinnecock Hills he held a two-shot lead with six holes to play, only to find himself intimidated by the fierce competitive stare of his playing partner Raymond Floyd, who would eventually overtake Stewart to win. A year later Payne was fourth behind Nick Faldo at Muirfield in 1987; his natural talent again short-changed by the lack of the mental skills needed to discipline his game.

Payne Stewart holes the vital birdie putt to win the 1989 US PGA Championship at Kemper Lakes, Chicago.

In 1988 Payne came to terms with this shortcoming and employed the services of a sports psychologist to help him produce the sort of golf he knew he was capable, and the results were dramatic. With maturity in his game, Payne birdied five of the last seven holes to overtake a faltering Mike Reid and win the US PGA Championship at Kemper Lakes in 1989. A second-place finish to an in-form Nick Faldo in the British Open at St Andrews in 1990 confirmed his new-found zest and self-belief under the pressure of major competition, and a year later he beat Scott Simpson in an 18-hole play-off to win his own national championship – the 1991 US Open at Hazeltine.

A star in stripes – with the 1991 US Open trophy at Hazeltine, Minneapolis.

With a distinctive swing reminiscent of the classic players of days gone by – and a dress sense to match – Payne Stewart enjoys a reputation as one of the game's most colourful characters.

The swing:
arms and body in balance

From a purely technical standpoint there are certainly better swings than this. But if we focus on the qualities of rhythm and tempo, few can better Payne Stewart's silky-smooth action. Pictures cannot do him justice, but Payne's swing is built around fine timing and synchronising the movement of the arms, the torso and the feet to produce a most repetitive, flowing motion.

Payne keeps his swing keys very simple. Basically, they revolve around the fundamentals of alignment, on maintaining a good posture, and repeating a smooth tempo and a consistent rhythm. With the driver he displays a comfortable address position (**1**), both arms relaxed and the left elbow looking at the target (a position it can be seen to maintain in the early stages of the swing). His hands are placed slightly behind the ball, which you will notice is well forward in his stance to encourage the proper upward sweeping motion of the clubhead through impact.

The initial movement of the club away from the ball is an interesting one (**2**). I would describe it as the butt-end of the club *leading* the head of the club, which for many players is a good image to keep in mind (too many amateurs are inclined to move the clubhead independently of everything else). You will notice initially that there is very little left forearm rotation. Payne draws the club away from the ball with a wide one-piece motion – the arm-and-shoulder triangle intact throughout.

Combined with the graceful turning motion of his right side, the late setting of the wrists results in a long and flowing backswing (**3**, **4**). Payne achieves an excellent extension of his arms away from his body to create a

1

2

3

4

relatively wide arc, the clubface pointing up towards the sky in a slightly closed position at the top. Then, with that wonderful lazy rhythm, he slides his lower body towards the target to signal the downswing. The lagging, flailing clubhead can be seen trying to catch up with the hands, which in turn are trying to catch up with the body (**5**). This is where Payne's acute sense of rhythm comes into play, as far as being able to co-ordinate this movement to a consistent impact position.

From the rear, we can see that as he meets the ball Payne keeps his right foot on the ground, but rolled inwards (**6**). His hips are open in relation to the target, yet his chest is fairly square to the ball, and his spine angle is now more erect than it was at address. All these points are explained by the fact that Payne employs an 'armsy' type release, (with the body resisting), as opposed to the body dominated type of action in which the upper body would be open and the spine angle consistent throughout.

Releasing the club with a free-flowing arm swing (**7**), Payne accelerates to a full finish, where as a result of his lateral hip motion towards the target he exhibits classic symptoms of the 'reverse-C', with his spine arched and his hands high (**8**).

This swing is very much in the mould of the classical swings of days gone by – what I would describe as a 'flail' type of action, featuring a late setting of the club near the top of the backswing, a down-cocking of the club as it changes direction and a full release as he whips the club through the ball.

Payne's action reminds me of someone cracking a whip. He makes a slow, deliberate wind-up, and then utilises the theory of centrifugal force being applied to the clubhead. And in so doing, he builds acceleration gradually.

5

6

7

8

What you can learn from Payne Stewart's swing

LESSON ONE: LATERAL MOVE
PROMOTES GOOD TURN, GREATER POWER

Keeping in mind a mental image of the way in which Payne Stewart starts his backswing is something that will benefit many golfers. A lateral motion of the right hip, combined with the thought of getting the butt-end of the club moving prior to the head, helps to get the swing off in the right sequence. Try this drill.

Place an old golf shaft or umbrella outside the edge of your right foot, as you see illustrated here. Then, as you rehearse the early stages of your backswing, sense that you move your right hip laterally towards the shaft (or umbrella) – 'bump' to the right. A good thought to have is that the butt-end of the club starts the backswing – this helps everything to move away together. Once you are able to repeat this initial movement, you can then focus on rotating your right side to reach the top of your backswing.

The benefit of this exercise is that it encourages fluency of motion, promotes a good weight shift and trains your hands and the clubhead to work in the proper sequence. It should also help to give you the feeling of having a little more 'snap' to your swing as you change direction and crack the clubhead like a whip through impact.

(2) Better footwork, better rhythm: If you tend to be a little flat-footed and generally static below the waist – as if your feet are set in concrete – this drill could help you. In the fashion of Payne Stewart, simply rolling your left foot in towards the right on the backswing, and your right foot towards the left on the downswing can really help in terms of promoting a better rhythm. Immediately it increases your awareness of the shifting of your weight back and forth, and allows you to recognise the fact that a golf swing requires a certain amount of motion.

Practise hitting half-shots with a short iron – set your swing to music.

LESSON TWO: SIMPLE DRILLS FOR A BETTER RHYTHM

Good rhythm and tempo with every club in the bag should be every golfer's goal. Here are two ways to help you achieve that.

(1) Continuous swinging for better tempo: Tee up six balls in a row, fairly close together, and then challenge yourself to hit one after the other in close succession. With a light grip pressure, strike the first ball, and then without too much thought or hesitation step up to the next ball and repeat the same rhythmical swing. Striking all six in this fashion promotes a good *flow* in your swing. The key is to maintain an even tempo and not exert too much effort. Think in terms of *swinging* the club, as opposed to *hitting* the balls.

CURTIS STRANGE

BORN: JANUARY 30TH, 1955, NORFOLK, VIRGINIA, USA. **TURNED PRO:** 1976. **HEIGHT:** 5ft 11in (1.8m).

Curtis Strange learned the game through his father, a golf professional from Norfolk, Virginia, who laid the groundwork, teaching and stressing to his son the importance of the fundamentals – how to grip the club and stand to the ball, how to turn his body and swing efficiently. He also instilled a sense of traditional values, and to this day Curtis is the model touring professional, with a grinding game that revolves around simple details and a clinical preparation in his shot-making.

From a young age, Curtis always dreamed of one day being a touring pro, and he nurtured his competitive instinct in combat with his twin brother, Allan. But it was Curtis who had the greater determination to succeed in golf, and following his victory in the South Eastern Amateur championship in 1973, he took a scholarship at Wake Forest University, in South Carolina. As a young man, Curtis was a very long hitter of the ball, and among his achievements he can list individual honours in the 1974 NCAA Championships, and a prominent performance in the victorious 1975 American Walker Cup team at St Andrews.

Things were different on tour. A man driven by perfection, Curtis found his swing to be lacking in the company of the world's top golfers, and it took several years before he could assert himself as a winner, which he did at the Pensacola Open in 1979. A keen student of the golf swing, he learned to use the bigger muscles in his body for control, and what he sacrificed in distance he more than made up for in accuracy. With his hands passive, Curtis focused on releasing the club with the right side of his body, maintaining his height through the shot and eliminating the 'reverse-C' look he had cultivated as a young player. As a result, he hit the ball as straight as an arrow, and in a four- year period from 1985, Curtis was the prolific money-winner on the US Tour, topping the money-list three times. In 1988 he became the first American to bank more than $1 million in a single season. But more important, he won his first major title, the US Open at Brookline.

Traditionally set up with narrow fairways, punishing rough and hard, fast greens, a typical US Open course demands Curtis Strange-like golf. It demands patience and a clinical strategy from

Sealed with a kiss – Curtis Strange wins his second US Open in 1989.

tee to green. It demands accuracy, and it demands nerve. Curtis proved to have these qualities in abundance when he defeated Nick Faldo in an 18-hole play-off at the Country Club, Brookline, in 1988. A year later he underlined his status as a new American superstar when he successfully defended that title at Oak Hill. At 35, he became the first winner of consecutive US Opens since Ben Hogan in 1950 and 1951.

Though his career has known its ups and downs, Curtis Strange remains one of the most calm and collected golfers of his generation. His game thrives on self-confidence and control, and once he finds the groove his scoring ability is electrifying. As a team player Curtis has represented the USA in four Ryder Cup matches, and in 1987, playing for America in the Dunhill Cup, he set a course record of 62 – 10 under par – round the Old Course at St Andrews.

Hard work has its rewards: Curtis Strange believes that, and has earned a well-deserved reputation as a man dedicated to reaching the top of his profession.

The swing:
turn, and turn again

Curtis' composed and neat looking address position sets the trend for his golf swing (**1**). His grip is one of those types that appear as if the club is moulded to his hands, albeit with his glove hand placed in a fairly weak position (showing just one knuckle). He has a fairly wide stance (you expect that in a body-controlled swing) and there is a

natural slant across his shoulders as the left is set slightly higher than the right.

Overall, a beautifully correct looking set-up position.

The tendency for his head and chest to move in tandem to the right with his hands and the club is evident right from the start (**2**). With that characteristic extension *off* the ball, Curtis hinges his wrists and sets the club relatively late in his backswing (**3**). Nothing is rushed, and that controlled

pace enables him to synchronise the swinging motion of his arms with the turning of his body.

Against the resistance in his knees and hips, he winds his upper body well behind the lower body, and if we were to extend a line up from his left hip, we would see just how far his upper body is behind his lower body. This certainly encourages a good weight shift, and a full turn with the upper body, which is particularly important with the

longer clubs.

Curtis' top of the backswing position is completed with a slight lifting of the arms, the left arm especially looking soft and relaxed (**4**). The club just appears to *settle* at the top of the backswing. He has a full wind up without any appreciable tension in his body. A noticeable feature of this backswing is the way that the toe of the clubhead hangs down in a fairly open position – a detail that accounts for the natural

1   2   3   4

left-to-right shape Curtis puts on his shots.

Having turned 'off the ball', Curtis must get his weight back to his left side, and he triggers his downswing with a noticeable 'kick-in' of the right knee (**5**), which gets his right side moving forward so he can get back to the ball at impact. In so doing, Curtis is able to keep his right side high through the shot, and get his right arm almost fully extended at impact (**6**). We can see how his arm position at impact is similar to that at address (which indicates he has kept the radius of his swing constant) and the fact his left hand is square to the line of the shot explains his consistency.

On a specific point, I know Curtis is aware of is the way his right knee tends to shoot out towards the ball approaching impact (as can be observed through the right foot raising up on the toe). Such a move can often disrupt the spine angle, and it forces Curtis to sometimes use his hands and arms more than he would like to square up his naturally open clubface. Having said that, great players like Curtis Strange have great hands, and he is able to make instinctive last minute adjustments to get the ball going in the right direction as his right side fires to a full finish (**7**, **8**).

Though he has reduced this in recent years, the lateral motion Curtis exhibits – moving his head and torso to the right on the backswing and to the left on the downswing – is very much a part of his natural timing. He swings the club with a beautiful pace and rhythm, and hits the ball with a controlled left-to-right shape.

The sheer repetitiveness of this swing explains why Curtis is especially well geared to US Open type courses where his poorer shots – normally a heel-cut – still finish in play. This is a key lesson: it is how good your *misses* are that ultimately determines your score.

5

6

7

8

What you can learn from Curtis Strange's swing

head will tend to move off the ball – particularly with the longer-shafted clubs. Curtis Strange proves the point that some movement of the head is perfectly acceptable, as long as it occurs *in conjunction with a good body turn*. Getting wound up behind the ball is an important aspect in solid ball-striking.

Freeing up your head so that it can move and rotate gently to the right as you turn your shoulders on the backswing enables you to transfer your weight correctly into your right side, which in turn encourages a positive weight shift towards the target on the downswing. This drill will help you to free up your head, so encouraging a proper turning motion.

LESSON ONE: FREE YOUR HEAD, TURN *BEHIND* THE BALL

Frankly, too many amateurs are fixated with keeping their head still. I see players who reward themselves with a weak reverse-pivot (above) for the simple reason they believe the head should remain rigidly in position. Wrong. In most good swings the

Place a pencil in your mouth, then take your regular set-up with a mid-iron and rehearse your backswing (left). Let your head rotate in tandem with your shoulders, and sense that your weight flows across into your right leg. As you reach the top of your swing, the pencil should point to the right of the ball, and you should be aware of looking at the ball out of your left eye.

Study your reflection in a mirror and make sure your upper body turns *behind* and is angled away from your lower body (measure this off from an imaginary line extended vertically from your left hip). Allowing your head to rotate will enable you to create a noticeable gap between the left shoulder and left hip at the top of your backswing – a positive sign of a good coiling action, and the perfect position from which to release the whole right side of your body through the ball.

LESSON TWO: RIGHT SIDE RELEASE IMAGES THROWING MOTION

Ben Hogan was once quoted as saying that he wished he had three right hands through impact. I agree with him: to maximise the force of your release, the right side of your body must play a very active part. Your golf swing should almost resemble a side- arm throwing motion. In throwing the ball you will notice that your right foot, knee, hip shoulder, arm and hand are all involved as your body rotates towards the target. As an exercise, throw a few balls, and then as you hit a few shots try to capture that same sensation of a powerful and committed right side release.

LEE TREVINO

BORN: DECEMBER 1ST 1939, DALLAS, TEXAS, USA. **TURNED PRO:** 1960. **HEIGHT:** 5ft 7in (1.7m)

The golf world has never known anyone quite like Lee Trevino. He is one who will go down in folklore. A self-made player; a rags-to-riches story. You can forget the typical script. Trevino is not one of those players who came up through the college system to assume his inevitable place in the rank and file of the touring pro. He lived in a small house without running water or electricity, dropped out of school at 14 to work at a driving range, and spent four years in the US Marines. At 21, he left to became the assistant pro at El Paso, in Texas, where he honed his unique swing to cope with the wind. And so was born one of the game's all-time great shot-makers.

But this is no hard-luck story. On the dusty baked plains of Texas, Lee also developed a hardened tenacity and a brash confidence in his game, largely through necessity. It was he who said, 'You don't know what pressure is until you play for five bucks when you only have two in your pocket', and the stories are endless about his gambling days and colourful younger years.

His fast tongue is matched by a sharp wit. Standing on the tee, waiting to get a play-off underway for the US Open at Merion, in 1971, Lee playfully tossed a rubber snake at Jack Nicklaus to relax the scene. More than anything else it relaxed *him*, and he went on to win the tournament, beating Nicklaus 68-71. Other players have other means to relieve tension; Trevino talks and acts the comedian. And his playful, laid-back approach to the game has entertained his millions of fans around the world.

With a smile almost as big as the trophy itself, Trevino wins the 1984 USPGA Championship.

Behind that bubbly exterior is a player with tremendous guts, skill, and a record to prove it. Lee won his first tournament in 1965 – the Texas State Open – and joined the tour full time in 1968. With total anonymity, in his rookie year he became the first player to shoot under 70 in all four rounds of the US Open, which he did at Oak Hill to equal Jack Nicklaus' previous record total of 275, and win his first major by four shots.

Straight driving and a clinical precision with the irons – matched only by his brilliant short game – would prove an equally potent combination overseas. Lee Trevino's swing may appear unorthodox, but it is relentlessly repetitive, and as a player he appreciates better than most that the object of this game is to get the ball *in the hole*. Capping a glorious summer in 1971 he won his first British Open at Royal Birkdale, and the following year successfully defended his title, holing from all over Scotland to crush Tony Jacklin at Muirfield. He would further add to his tally of majors with victories in the US PGA Championship in 1974, and again in 1984 at the age of 44.

Struck by lightning at the Western Open in 1976, Lee has suffered back trouble ever since, and yet the colour and zest he brings to the game is without comparison. More than perhaps any other player he just loves to play golf. A long line of doctors have told him that in the past he worked himself too hard, and beat too many balls. So, with a medical excuse to take things easy, Lee Trevino joined his friends on the senior tour in 1990, where, his golf ever as sharp as his mind, he won seven times in his debut season. Rumour has it he hits more balls now than he ever did.

Famous for his stories of gambling $5 when he only had $2 in his pocket, Lee Trevino will go down in history, not only as one of the game's great players, but as one of its most colourful characters.

The swing:
aim left, hit straight

Lee Trevino's swing is certainly self-taught, but if you close your eyes and listen to the strike as the clubhead enters the turf, you'd quickly appreciate his natural skill. For my money, Lee's swing is the epitome of a passive-hands type release through impact. He keeps the clubhead extending down the target line longer than anybody in the game, which explains his

radar-like accuracy. Lee's natural shot is a fade, which he controls with a low trajectory, but in recent years he has worked also on moving the ball from right to left.

Lee sets up with his feet, knees and hips aligned well to the left of the target – the shoulders a little less so (**1**). Looking face on, the left arm and clubshaft form one straight line, and the ball *appears* well back (though given Lee's characteristically open stance this is a little deceiving to the eye). We

can see a few knuckles on Lee's left-hand grip, and he forms a definite trigger with the index finger of his right hand. This trigger helps the right hand to hold the clubface square through impact, and keep it from rolling over.

In starting the swing, Lee moves the club out and away from the ball, primarily with his arms and upper body (**2**). There is no rotation of the club starting back, as the unit of his arms,

shoulders and chest move away together, the clubface being slightly closed for the first few feet of its journey. You will also notice there is very little in the way of a hinging motion in the wrists: as the swing progresses, the right elbow folds and the club works upwards as he winds against a very resistant lower body (**3**). As he reaches the top of his swing, the gradual inward flexing of the

1

2

3

4

right wrist (accompanied by the bowing of the left) places the club is a short, shut, laid-off position – pretty much matching the alignment of his body (**4**).

On the way back, Lee creates a good deal of torque with this upper body wind-up over a minimal hip turn. Look at how tight his shirt is over the middle part of his back – this reflects the coiling action of the big back muscles. Starting down he then makes a distinct lateral movement with his knees, immediately dropping his right elbow in towards his side (**5**). At the same time, the right shoulder can be seen to work *down and under*.

And now for Trevino's trademark: look at the way he re-routes the club with a distinctive loop, the clubhead dropping behind him as the plane of his swing shallows. This strong right-sided move – linked with the fact that he maintains his spine angle – is what enables Lee to keep the clubhead moving on line to and past impact (**6**).

When viewing Trevino down the line it is remarkable also how the angle of the clubshaft at impact mirrors the angle at address – copybook stuff. And look at how squarely he maintains the clubface even though the ball has long gone (**7**) – no wonder he has such great control.

Trevino's swing is what I would describe as an 'upper body release'. Look at the way he commits himself to staying *down* on the shot as the hips unwind and his arms extend the club out towards the target. And that horizontal finish typifies a body-release type of player (**8**).

Of course, these pictures do not reveal adequately the speed and rhythm of Lee's action. Because he is so on line coming into the ball, he can afford to be very aggressive. There is no wasted motion in this swing. It is efficient and direct – just like the man himself.

5

6

7

8

What you can learn from Lee Trevino's swing

LESSON ONE: RE-ROUTE
DOWNSWING PATH FOR INSIDE ATTACK
Generally speaking, it is true to say that golfers slice as a result of the path of their downswing being too far outside the path of their backswing. In other words, the club cuts badly across the ball, approaching on much too steep an angle, which, particularly when combined with an open clubface, creates left-to-right spin.

It appears these golfers loop the club from the outside when they swing down. One way to counter this is to *reverse* the loop, and copy Trevino's action.

Despite what you have probably heard about standing closed or aiming to the right to encourage a hook and eliminate a slice, doing the opposite is actually more effective. When you stand open, you can swing the club back on your body line and then *re-route* it back down on the target line – much like Lee. This encourages a more in-to-out path, a shallower plane, and, if you release your hands – i.e. let them cross over through impact – you should draw the ball. [Lee fades the ball because he holds the face slightly open through impact with a firm right hand.]

With a middle iron, take your fairly open stance and keep the picture of Lee's loop in your mind. Swing the club back along the line of your toes, complete your backswing, then re-route the club down on an inside path (as you see illustrated) until you sense you are able to approach the ball consistently from the inside.

From the top, the key is to focus on the movement of your right shoulder. As Trevino does, encourage your right shoulder to work *down and under* as your downswing begins – not out and around. Before long you will find that doing this enables you to approach the ball on a more in-to-out path, and if you release your hands the ball should move from right to left.

Put a couple of clubs down to assist in your alignment, one relating to your target, the other to remind you of your open body position. After practising this move for a while, and grooving the correct loop, you will be able to return to a more orthodox set-up position and yet still retain the same feeling of releasing the club from the inside.

LESSON TWO: MAINTAIN SPINE ANGLE, HANDS LOW THROUGH THE BALL

Characteristic of all good ball-strikers is the consistency of their spine angle from address through to impact, and again Trevino makes for an interesting case study. He is a master craftsman with the irons for the simple reason he returns the clubface squarely to the ball with a swing that revolves around controlled body angles.

One way to practise this skill – and this really is as much a mental exercise as it is physical – is to imagine that as you set up to the ball with a good posture you rest your rear on a chair (as you see illustrated above), and then maintain that angled look as much as you can up until the moment of impact. After the ball has gone you will naturally straighten up as you swing through to the finish.

Prior to impact there must be no raising of the upper body or straightening of the legs – in short, no erroneous movement which threatens to disrupt your body angles and thus the position of the clubface. At the moment of impact, the angle of your spine – and indeed the plane of the shaft – should mirror the position you set at address. For accurate and consistent ball-striking, especially with the irons, that's your ultimate goal.

TOM WATSON

BORN: SEPTEMBER 4TH, 1949, KANSAS CITY, MISSOURI, USA. **TURNED PRO:** 1971. **HEIGHT:** 5ft 9in (1.7m).

At the time of writing, there is only one major title Tom Watson has not won – the US PGA Championship. In a career spanning three decades, the straight-talking psychology major from Stanford University has aspired to the upper reaches of golf's monarchy, one of the game's all-time greats, and perhaps the only player of his generation who could truly rival Jack Nicklaus in his prime.

Tom has always been a long, pure hitter of the golf ball. In that respect he gets better with age, for in my opinion he is in his forties a more impressive and consistent ball-striker than he was in the days he was busy winning major championships. At 5ft 9in, Tom is no giant, but a powerful build and Popeye-like forearm muscles yield a brisk swing that matches his forthright attitudes on the game and indeed on life itself. Statistically he remains one of the most consistent players in the world from tee to green. In his prime, he was one of the all-time great pressure-putters, but increasingly the years bring only fleeting glimpses of his past glory. If his putting had aged only half as well, there is no question in my mind he would still be one of the most dominant players of the 1990's.

The Old Claret Jug buckled under the heat; Watson didn't, winning his fifth Open title at Royal Birkdale in 1983.

A traditionalist in every sense of the word, Tom is driven not by money, but by the history and integrity of the game he loves so dearly. In his era of greatness, between 1975 and 1984, he won a total of eight major championships and was six times voted PGA Player of the Year. More significantly, in four of those majors, he duelled head-to-head with Jack Nicklaus – at the 1977 and 1981 US Masters, the 1977 British Open, and the 1982 US Open at Pebble Beach. In the latter, his outrageous chip-in from tangly rough beside the 71st green would be remembered as the shot of the decade.

A youthful looking man, Tom's implacable demeanour rarely changes. Whether he is shooting 65 or 75, he conducts himself in the manner befitting one of the game's most respected statesmen, and that spirit is appreciated wherever he plays. In Britain he is especially at home with the natives, his haul of five Open championships a testament to his love affair with the traditional windy challenge of links golf. Tom simply enjoys good golf – and particularly the Old Course at Ballybunion. So far he has only tinkered in course design, but in the years to come his vision as an architect will surely leave as great an impression as his genius as a golfer.

The no-nonsense style of Tom Watson has yielded five Open championships, two Masters and a US Open. Quite simply, the boy from Kansas is a legend of the game he loves so dearly.

The swing:

brisk arms, active body

Tom Watson's swing is very much a combination of a speedy arm swing synchronised with a flowing, active body motion. He has superb hand-eye co-ordination and any technical flaws in his golf swing are overcome by an instinctive awareness for the clubhead. When he is swinging well, every shot comes right out of the middle of the clubface. A high-ball hitter, he plays with a controlled and natural right-to-left shape, although he is an artist at hitting different shape shots.

With a driver, Tom looks to be in a 'ready' position at address, and his body angles have a sharp look to them (**1**). His weight is centred over the balls of his feet, slightly favouring the right side. With a fairly strong right-hand grip (we can see that the 'V' formed between thumb and forefinger points towards his right shoulder), Tom makes one or two customary waggles, then it's off to the races.

As he moves the club away from the ball we then see an early hinging up of the wrists (**2**) – a Watson trademark. Against a braced right knee he turns his upper body away from the target until the shaft is simultaneously horizontal with the ground and parallel with the line across his toes. From here on the shoulders can be seen to continue to turn on a relatively flat plane while the arms make a noticeable upward lifting motion to the top (**3**).

Combined with Tom's strong right-hand grip, this upright swing produces a slightly bowed left wrist position and a closed clubface at the top – as witnessed looking down the line (**4**).

From this fully wound up backswing position, in which the

1 2 3 4

shoulders have turned at least twice as far as the hips, Tom now begins his movement forward with a planting of the left heel (**5**). As his weight moves towards the target there is a distinct downward pulling motion of the club with the arms. This weight transfer and arm motion happen *together,* and it appears that gravity is pulling the club down towards the ball.

It's a chain reaction: the left side of his body clears out of the way, and he stays down on the shot superbly well as the arms swing the clubhead through impact, and his head remains steady behind the ball (**6**). One of Tom's big swing keys is to maintain his spine angle back and through and to keep his hands low through impact. We can see here that he still has some work to do in that department, as his hands are still fairly high – in golf, one's work is never done!

Brought up in an era when players were taught to drive the legs and yet stay behind the ball, there are occasionally remnants of these theories in Tom's swing, notably a slight 'reverse-C' in his back as he extends the clubhead through the ball (**7**). Generally speaking, any problems in his swing stem from a tendency to be a little too aggressive with his lower body, and when his lower body gets too far ahead of his hands and arms he loses the timing of his release. His hands and arms then have to play 'catch-up' through impact, which is why Tom is susceptible to hitting the odd block or hook.

But when the two halves of his body unwind in sync, his reward is the ability to release the club as hard as he likes knowing that he will strike the ball solidly down the fairway – and of course wrap it all up with that full, unmistakable Tom Watson finish (**8**).

5

6

7

8

What you can learn from Tom Watson's swing

approach. Golfers either freeze over the ball, or their movement is inconsistent. What you need is a cast-iron, pre-shot routine for consistency. Ultimately, you want the time it takes from the moment you pull the club from the bag up until the time you strike the ball to be consistent – with every club in the bag.

Do your best to discipline your game along these lines. As you arrive at the ball, study the situation and try to picture the flight of the shot in your mind. Then, as you assume your set-up position, waggle the club as you fix you eyes on the target, take aim and be ready to swing. With possibly one final glance and waggle, make your swing.

Working on this type of pre-shot routine not only gives you something positive to focus on, it helps to eliminate tension under pressure. In terms of your natural tempo, the key is to match your waggle with the rhythm of your swing. Experiment to find a system of waggling the clubhead that suits your style.

Remember the old saying: *'As ye waggle, so shall ye swing'*.

LESSON ONE: 'AS YE WAGGLE, SO SHALL YE SWING'

Though this cannot ever fully be appreciated in pictures, Tom Watson follows a pre-shot routine you could set your watch by. Once he arrives at the ball, he finalises his yardage, takes aim on the target, waggles the club, and then fires. I doubt his rhythm has skipped a beat since the day Tom first picked up a club.

This 'routine factor' is important in golf. I see too many players who are careless in their

LESSON TWO: CO-ORDINATE ARMS AND BODY IN HARMONY

Although Tom uses a lot of 'body' in his swing, I want you to focus on how aggressively he uses his arms, particularly through impact. Fundamental to my teaching philosophy is the importance of blending the arm swing with the body turn – which Tom does beautifully – and one of the easiest ways to do this is practise with your feet close together, about 6-9 inches apart.

In too many cases – and this applies particularly to those golfers who are prone to slicing the ball – the body is so far out of position that the arms are never given the opportunity to swing freely and *release* the clubhead through impact. This is why this exercise is so effective: with your balance under threat, the emphasis is on *turning* your body and *swinging* your arms in harmony.

As you hit shots with a short iron, the key is to turn your upper body away from the target, and let your arms swing up accordingly. Then simply unwind your body and accelerate your arms and the clubhead *through* the ball. With your feet close together it's

difficult to be overly aggressive with your body, but as long as you retain a good balance and keep them tension free, you *can* be aggressive with your arms. Get the blend of arms and body right, and watch how straight the ball flies.

IAN WOOSNAM

BORN: MARCH 2ND, 1958, OSWESTRY, ENGLAND. **TURNED PRO:** 1976. **HEIGHT:** 5ft 4in (1.6m).

In 1987, feisty Welshman Ian Woosnam was the most successful player in the world, winning eight tournaments and netting more than $1m in prize money. He became the first British player to win the World Matchplay championship, beating his European rivals Nick Faldo, Seve Ballesteros and Sandy Lyle in succession, won the European Order of Merit, and rounded off the year with a fine solo performance in the World Cup in Hawaii, to take both the individual and team honours for Wales.

The son of a farmer, Ian Woosnam's golf is of the aggressive, street-fighting variety. He attributes his ability to power the ball with such nonchalant ease to his great upper body strength, the legacy of childhood days spent bundling bales of hay and driving the tractor. A brash competitive spirit comes naturally. Five foot, four inches in his spikes, the boy who grew up in the small town of Oswestry in the borders between England and Wales, developed one of the prettiest swings in the modern game, and hits the ball an incredible distance for a man of his size. His swing, at best, looks easy, but harnessing that power has taken time and patience.

Taking the 1988 PGA trophy at Wentworth.

After a brief amateur career, which included county honours with Shropshire as a team-mate of Sandy Lyle, Ian turned professional in 1976, at the age of 18, and has earned respect the hard way. It took three visits to the qualifying school before he gained his place on the European tour, whereupon he bought a camper-van and toured the continent, often sleeping in his waterproofs to keep warm. Life was a struggle. In his first five years he won a little over £6,000, and there were times when he considered packing it all

Time to party – Woosnam bravely holes the winning putt to become US Masters champion at Augusta in 1991.

in. But his pride and determination drove him forward, and as his game matured he learned how to convert a natural ball-striking ability into consistent low scoring. The breakthrough came in 1982, winning the World Under-25 title and the prestigious Swiss Open. With that taste of success, Woosie's hunger grew.

Hugely powerful, Ian Woosnam's charmingly free and rhythmic action reflects his outlook on life. Probably because he finds the act of hitting the golf ball so simple, he has never been technically minded. He is a natural player who survives chiefly on feel and intuition, and when he finds a positive forward gear has the game to demolish all around him. His natural flow and rhythm are stymied at times when his lower back problems become acute, and as with many travel-weary, ball-beating tour players of the modern era, he has to play in pain at times.

At his best, however, Woosie is a strong, gutsy competitor with a propensity to reel off birdies one after another, and he excites the crowd with his easy power. His true colours were never more evident than at Augusta in 1991. In the thick of a partisan crowd, and needing a four at the last to win the title, Woosie buckled down to business, smashing his driver to fly the ball clean over the bunker on the 18th – a carry of some 270 yards. The curling eight footer he then holed for his first major championship underlined perfectly his pugnacious fighting character.

Although a diminutive figure, Ian Woosnam possesses one of the game's prettiest swings and with it is one of the world's longest hitters.

The swing:
turn back, and rip it!

In short, this is a very simple swing. Ian works on turning back, getting his weight behind the ball, and giving it a good whack with the hands. His swing is very much geared around balance – certainly with strong short legs his centre of gravity is very low, which enables him to retain such good balance and hit the ball hard. He makes an excellent turn and creates

tremendous torque with very little wasted motion. When you add those things together – and also take into account his strong forearms – it is easy to see why he is such a good striker of the ball.

At address we can see that Ian stands fairly upright to the ball, with minimal flex in the knees (**1**). His arms just hang from his shoulders in a very natural manner, and he has a classic grip, in every sense of the word. As far as alignment is concerned, he

favours standing a little closed (aiming to the right) with his feet. This position assists the right side of his body in turning out of the way on the backswing.

Starting the club back, Ian makes a simple movement away with the arms, hands and shoulders for the first few feet of the swing (**2**) – which we see clearly down the line. And then, with wonderful simplicity, the right side of his body (i.e. the right hip and right shoulder) makes an

emphatic turning motion as he cocks the wrists (**3**) and continues his backswing movement.

For a short man Woosie swings the club on a fairly upright plane. He makes a very full backswing, with his left shoulder turned all the way under his chin (**4**). [His back must have been in pretty good shape when this sequence was taken because he makes this full turn without lifting his left heel up off the ground.] He is fully 'loaded up' with his body at

1   2   3   4

the top, and yet a good thing to note is how *soft* his arms appear – look at the 'kink' in his left arm. Note also that the club is swung a fraction across the line at the top, a position which encourages his natural draw.

Though the pictures fail to show this clearly, a common factor in all good swings is that the lower body is starting to move forwards while for a split-second the arms and the club are still completing their backswing movement. Woosie's action is a perfect example: moving in two directions at once increases the *leverage* in his swing, and as he gets his legs into a solid 'sit-down' position, he is packed with power (**5**).

This two-directional movement at the top actually increases the wrist-cock as Woosie's hands swing down, and creates the situation in which the clubhead can be seen to be lagging well behind the hands coming into impact. A whip-like action then occurs as the left leg straightens up to support the hit, and Woosie smashes the ball with his right hand as the club whistles through (**6**).

Note that immediately after impact his right forearm has rolled over his left and the knuckles on the back of his left hand are facing the ground (**7**) – again, this 'crossover' explains his natural right-to-left shape.

Woosie's swing reminds me of a door that is open and then slams shut through impact.

Although his hips are open, he is more of a hands-and-arms release type of player, as opposed to the modern body-release type player. This is indicated by the fact that his hands appear to be working independently away from his body after the ball has been struck. The consistency of this action is reliant on timing, rhythm, and good balance. Woosie has these skills in abundance – as he demonstrates with this super statuesque finish (**8**).

5

6

7

8

What you can learn from Ian Woosnam's swing

TURN RIGHT SIDE OUT OF THE WAY, THEN FIRE!

The simple philosophy that Ian follows would really help many players: turn the right side out of the way on the backswing and then release the club with the forearms through impact. Someone once described his swing as 'two turns and a swish', and that's a good thought to keep in mind.

An easy way to encourage your right side to turn out of the way on the backswing is to stand with your feet slightly closed at address (opposite page). Keep your shoulders and hips square to the target line and pull your right foot back a few inches. Doing this will free up the whole right side of your body, and enable you to complete your backswing turn while swinging the arms up to the top. Your key thoughts should be to turn your right hip pocket behind you and to turn your chest on *top* of your right leg. You are now in a position where you can swing down from the inside and freely release the club.

To further promote the right-to-left shape that Ian Woosnam has with all his shots – and this will certainly give you more distance – turn your right side out of the way on the backswing, then *slam the door* (i.e. the clubface) shut by rotating your right forearm over your left through the impact area, as you see illustrated here (right). Immediately after contact is made, it should feel as if the back of your left hand is facing the ground. With a little practise, this combination of a closed stance and right forearm release should enable you to draw the ball.

Particularly with the longer clubs, many top players stand with their feet slightly closed, the reason being that your feet are not that important in the overall context of your body alignment, and yet such a stance can and will help you to make a full turn.

ACKNOWLEDGEMENTS

ADDITIONAL PICTURE CREDITS

p6 Simon Bruty

p10l David Rogers, p11 Gary Newkirk

p28l Mike Cooper, p28r Stephen Munday

p29 Rusty Jarrett

p34r Simon Bruty

p41 Gary Newkirk

p46l Stephen Munday

p52l Rusty Jarrett

p53 Gary Newkirk

p58 Mike Hewitt

p64l + r Stephen Munday

p65 J.D. Cuban

p70r David Rogers

p71 J.D. Cuban

p82l Steve Powell

p83 Tony Duffy

p88l Stephen Munday, p88r J.D. Cuban

p89 Phil Cole

p94l J.D. Cuban, p94r Simon Bruty

100l Phil Cole, p100r Stephen Munday

p106l Gary Newkirk, p106r Steve Powell

p107 Stephen Munday

p112l Simon Bruty

p118 Stephen Munday

p124l Rusty Jarrett, p124r Stephen Munday

p125 Simon Bruty

p136l J.D. Cuban

p137 Gary Newkirk

p148r Anton Want

Sequences of Daly, Trevino and Floyd: Leonard Kamsler
Sequences of Norman and Mickelson: J.D. Cuban
Sequences of Nicklaus: courtesy of Jack Nicklaus